From the Frio
to Del Rio

Number Twenty-Eight: Tarleton State University
Southwestern Studies in the Humanities
T. Lindsay Baker, General Editor

ATMX travel guides

From the Frio to Del Rio

Travel Guide to the

WESTERN HILL COUNTRY AND THE LOWER PECOS CANYONLANDS

Mary S. Black

Texas A&M University Press College Station

First edition

This paper meets the requirements of ANSI/NISO Z39.48-1992 (Permanence of Paper).
Binding materials have been chosen for durability.
Manufactured in China by Everbest Printing Co.
through FCI Print Group

LIBRARY OF CONGRESS CATALOGING-IN-PUBLICATION DATA

Names: Black, Mary S., 1946– author.
Title: From the Frio to Del Rio: travel guide to the southwestern Hill Country and the Lower Pecos / Mary S. Black.
Description: First edition. | College Station: Texas A&M University Press, [2017] | Includes bibliographical references and index.
Identifiers: LCCN 2016030144 (print) | LCCN 2016031033 (ebook) | ISBN 9781623495084 (flex with flaps: alk. paper) | ISBN 9781623495091 (ebook)
Subjects: LCSH: Texas—Guidebooks. | Texas, South—Guidebooks. | Texas, West—Guidebooks. | Texas Hill Country (Tex.)—Guidebooks. | Trans-Pecos (Tex. and N.M.)—Guidebooks.
Classification: LCC F384.3 .B55 2017 (print) | LCC F384.3 (ebook) | DDC 917.6404—dc23
LC record available at https://lccn.loc.gov/2016030144

A list of titles in this series is available at the end of the book.

Contents

1. Introduction to Southwest Texas 1
   - Western Hill Country 4
   - Lower Pecos Canyonlands 7

2. Natural Environment 20
   - Western Hill Country 20
   - Lower Pecos Canyonlands 26

3. State Parks and Other Public Recreation Areas 38
   - Amistad National Recreation Area 38
   - Devils River State Natural Area 41
   - Devil's Sinkhole State Natural Area 42
   - Garner State Park 44
   - Lost Maples State Natural Area 51
   - Kickapoo Cavern State Park 54
   - Seminole Canyon State Park and Historic Site 58

4. Rock Art 61

5. Historic Forts 72
   - Fort Clark 72
   - Fort Duncan 77
   - Fort Inge 78

6. Hunting 81

7. Towns 87
   - Barksdale 88
   - Brackettville 89
   - Camp Wood 95
   - Comstock 101

Concan 103
Del Rio 111
Eagle Pass 128
El Indio 136
Leakey 136
Normandy 143
Quemado 143
Rocksprings 144
Utopia 148
Uvalde 152
Vanderpool 165

8. Ghost Towns 169

Carta Valley 170
Devils River 170
Dolores 170
Juno 171
Laguna 172
Langtry 172
Montell 176
Pumpville 177
Shumla 179

9. Scenic Routes 180

Twisted Sisters Trail 180
Bullhead Canyon Trail 182
Buffalo Soldiers and Black Seminole Indian Scouts Trail 182
New Money and Old Art Trail 182
Bat Trail 183
Aviation History Trail 184
Great Train Robbery Trail 185
Pecos Crossing Trail 186
Chihuahuan Trail 187
Dead Man's Trail 193

10. Movies 197

You Can Help 201
Tricky Travel Trivia 203
For Further Reading 207
Index 209

From the Frio
to Del Rio

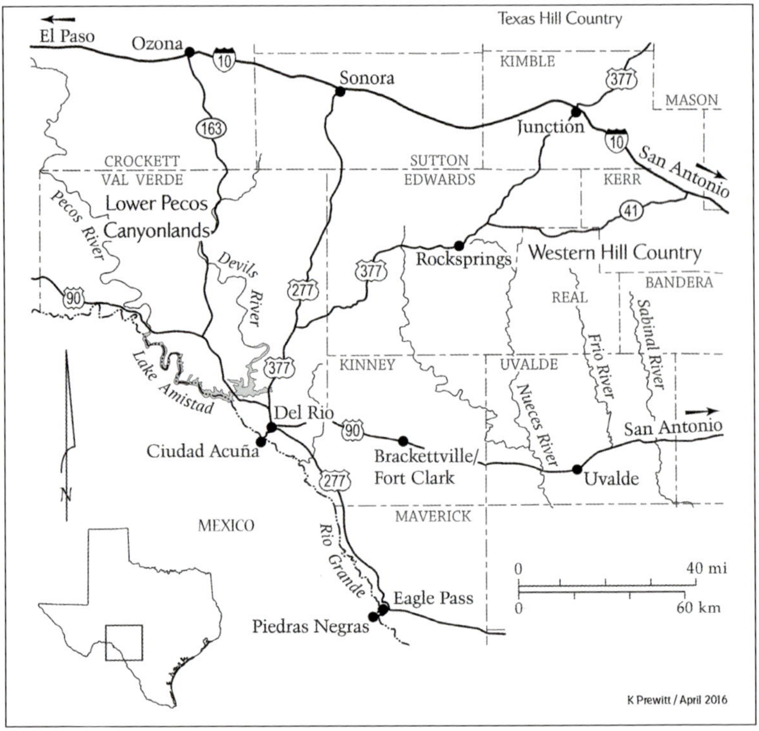

Southwest Texas

Southwest Texas spreads out in the glow of sunset. Photo by Thomas C. Self.

1

Introduction to Southwest Texas

Most of Southwest Texas is off the beaten path, but the region offers visitors some of the most striking scenery in the state with spring-fed rivers, twisting limestone canyons, and soaring hilltop vistas. The region also offers unforgettable outdoor adventures for travelers in Texas. Camping, fishing, and hunting are some of the most popular activities, but visitors can also explore prehistoric Native American rock art and historic forts that protected the frontier. There are ghost towns to discover and canyons to hike. Visitors can splash into water sports and empty dust out of their boots all in the same day. Whether you are riding the "Twisted Sisters" on your motorcycle or blasting full-throttle out US 90 toward Big Bend, you'll find plenty of reasons to stop and appreciate the trail in this guide.

Southwest Texas as conceived here is a small region spanning some 125 miles east to west and 75 miles north to south. It begins about 50 miles west of San Antonio along the Sabinal River, one of a series of south-flowing, spring-fed rivers draining the western Edwards Plateau. Heading west, one encounters the Sabinal, Frio, Nueces, Devils, and Pecos Rivers, each flowing southward.

For travelers, Southwest Texas lies to the south of I-10 and north of US 90. The easternmost town is Utopia on the Sabinal River, and the westernmost is Langtry on the Rio Grande not far from its junction with the Pecos River. There are only three small cities in the region, Uvalde, Eagle Pass, and Del Rio, all on the southern edge.

Fewer than 200,000 people live in Southwest Texas, which is largely rural. The modern settling of Southwest Texas started with a string of US Army forts in 1849. Black Americans or "Buffalo Soldiers" served at these forts after the Civil War, and Black Seminoles were hired as Indian scouts in the 1870s. Comanche and Apache Indians and other tribes fought for this land, which had been theirs for centuries, as newcomers encroached. Kickapoo Indians still live along the Rio Grande today. Italian immigrants started vineyards and built stone buildings in Del Rio during the 1880s. Chinese workers and German, Irish, and Mexican immigrants came to build the southern route of the transcontinental railroad in 1880s. The story of these people and their adaptation to the land is full of grit and color.

Southwest Texas occupies the southwestern Edwards Plateau, a karstic limestone expanse. Through geological time rainwater has eroded the porous limestone, leaving deep canyons and steep, hilly terrain on the surface and many sinkholes, caves, and crevices underground. Southwest Texas is on the northeastern edge of the vast Chihuahuan Desert, which stretches west to Arizona and south deep into Mexico. This helps explain why rainfall drops off precipitously from east to west across Southwest Texas, from 32 inches annually at Utopia to less than half that amount at Langtry (15 inches). To the east there are many more trees, especially along the rivers, and even the hills are covered in oak and juniper (cedar). To the west trees are smaller and a lot fewer except along the rivers. The upland terrain is covered in sage and creosote, a low bush that exudes a tarry resin used to preserve railroad ties and an indicator species for the Chihuahuan Desert.

Southwest Texas can be thought of as having two subregions, the Western Hill Country and the Lower Pecos Canyonlands because of differing natural environments and history. Driving through the Lower Pecos Canyonlands, people need sunglasses all year round because of the white, reflective quality of earth and air, but traveling through the Western Hill Country brings drivers into the deep shadows of giant oaks and cypress trees near crisp, flowing streams.

Emergency Information

Dial 911 for emergency services—ambulance, fire, police.

If you need medical attention while in these areas, please go to the nearest hospital in Del Rio, Uvalde, or Eagle Pass. Pharmacies are also located in these towns. San Antonio has the nearest large medical facilities, but it is 1.5 hours from Uvalde and over 3 hours from Del Rio.

Val Verde Regional Medical Center
801 N. Bedell Ave. (east of Veteran's Blvd., or US 90)
Del Rio, TX 78840
830–775–8566
www.vvrmc.org

Val Verde Regional Medical Center is a Joint Commission–accredited, ninety-three-bed, level IV trauma center. In addition to emergency services, there is a walk-in clinic open Wednesday through Friday, 11:00 a.m. to 8:00 p.m.; Saturdays, 10:00 a.m. to 6:00 p.m.; and Sundays, 1:00 to 5:00 p.m. The clinic is located at 1200 N. Bedell Avenue at 10th Street.

Uvalde Memorial Hospital
1195 Garner Field Rd. (FM 1023)
Uvalde, TX 78801
830–278–3086
www.umhtx.org

Uvalde Memorial Hospital is a Joint Commission–accredited, sixty-six-bed, not-for-profit county hospital serving five counties. Top-of-the-line equipment provides the service region with access to the latest medical technology. Located just off East Main Street on FM 1023 just about a block past the "Y" with US 90.

Fort Duncan Regional Medical Center
3333 N. Foster Maldonado Blvd. (off US 277 and US 57)
Eagle Pass, TX 78852
830–773–5321
www.fortduncanmedicalcenter.com

Fort Duncan Regional Medical Center is a Joint Commission–accredited, 101-bed, level IV trauma center. The emergency Department has fourteen beds.

The Western Hill Country

In the Western Hill Country, rivers and streams sparkle in the sunlight, and huge trees open their arms in welcome. Limestone cliffs rise above the rivers for dramatic landscapes. Bigtooth maples and yellow sycamores brighten

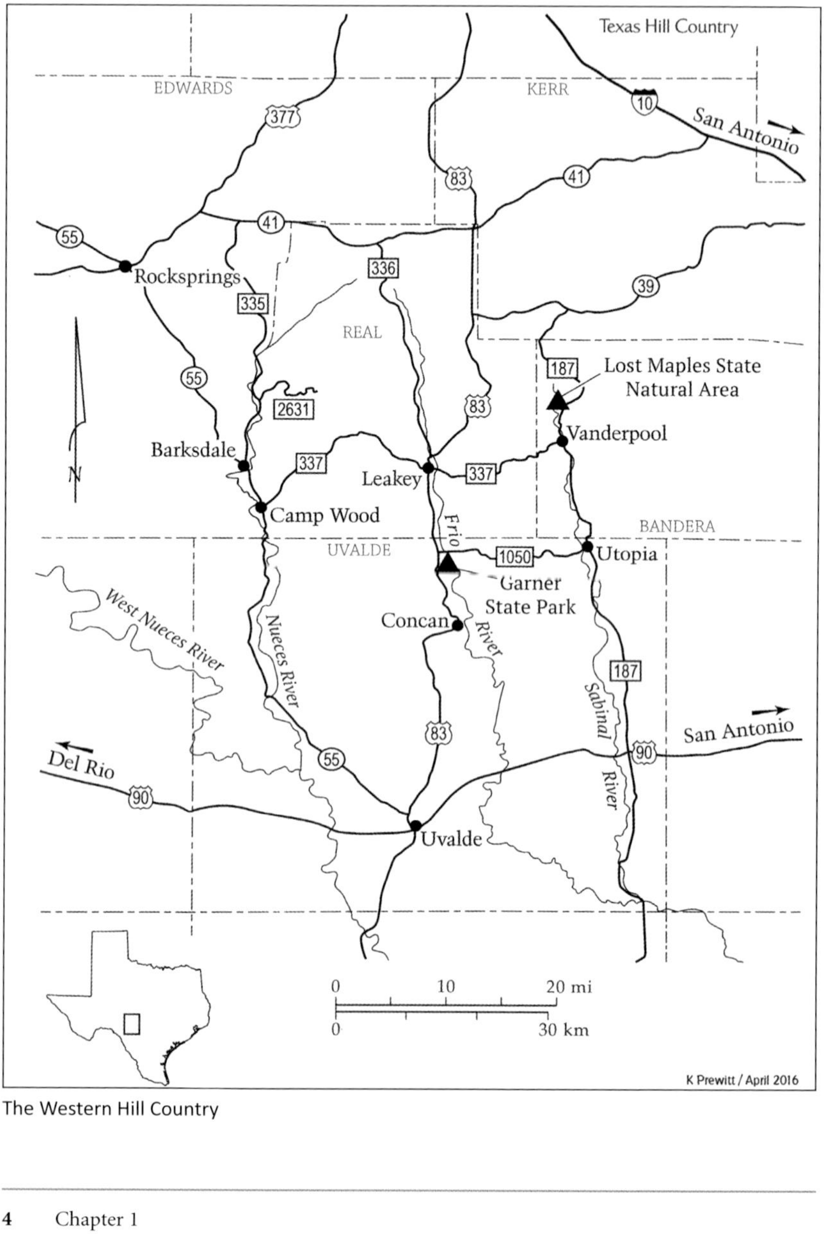

The Western Hill Country

the canyons in fall. Small, winding roads snake through the region, which is home to many summer cabins and resorts.

The Western Hill Country lies less than 100 miles from San Antonio or Del Rio and only 168 miles from Austin. The area is on the western edge of the greater Texas Hill Country, and thus its name. The clear, cool waters of the Nueces, the Frio, and the Sabinal Rivers bubble up from springs on the Edwards Plateau and cut down through the Western Hill Country, making this area ideal for recreation. Nearly one million visitors a year attest to its attractions.

Summer is the most popular time to visit the Western Hill Country because of the many opportunities for water sports on the cold, clear rivers. Hundreds of thousands of people come to Garner State Park or Lost Maples State Natural Area to enjoy the natural beauty. Kayakers and "tubers" splash in the Frio as it runs to join the Nueces in Southeast Texas. Motorcyclists wind through the Twisted Sisters and stop for some of the best barbecue in the state in Leakey or Concan. Sportsmen come to hunt and fish, and antiquers prowl through shops in Uvalde or Utopia. Each fall the road near Vanderpool is packed with "leaf peepers" who have come to view the brilliant color of a hidden stand of bigtooth maples.

Streams flow through the Western Hill Country from upland springs. Photo by Thomas C. Self.

Human beings have lived in the river canyons for thousands of years, but because of the relatively wet environment, few artifacts remain. Any rock art that might have been painted here is long gone except for a few painted pebbles. Native American peoples hunted and made camps everywhere in the Western Hill Country, however, and some remained until the 1870s. American and other settlers arrived in the 1850s, but few permanent settlements arose until after the Civil War (1860–64).

Limestone forms majestic formations in the Lower Pecos Canyonlands. Photo by Thomas C. Self.

There are hundreds of options for vacation lodging in the Western Hill Country. This guide makes no attempt to list them all but instead gives you several websites that aggregate listings for cabins, lodges, and RV parks:

www.friolodging.com
www.hillcountryrivers.com
www.friorivervacationrentals.com
www.friocanyonchamber.com
www.backroadstexas.net
www.homeaway.com/vacation-rentals/texas/leakey/r7158
www.clearspringslodging.com

The Lower Pecos Canyonlands

The land itself can look intimidating. Generally hot and dry, winds often blow 30–40 miles per hour. Most topsoil is gone, leaving exposed limestone

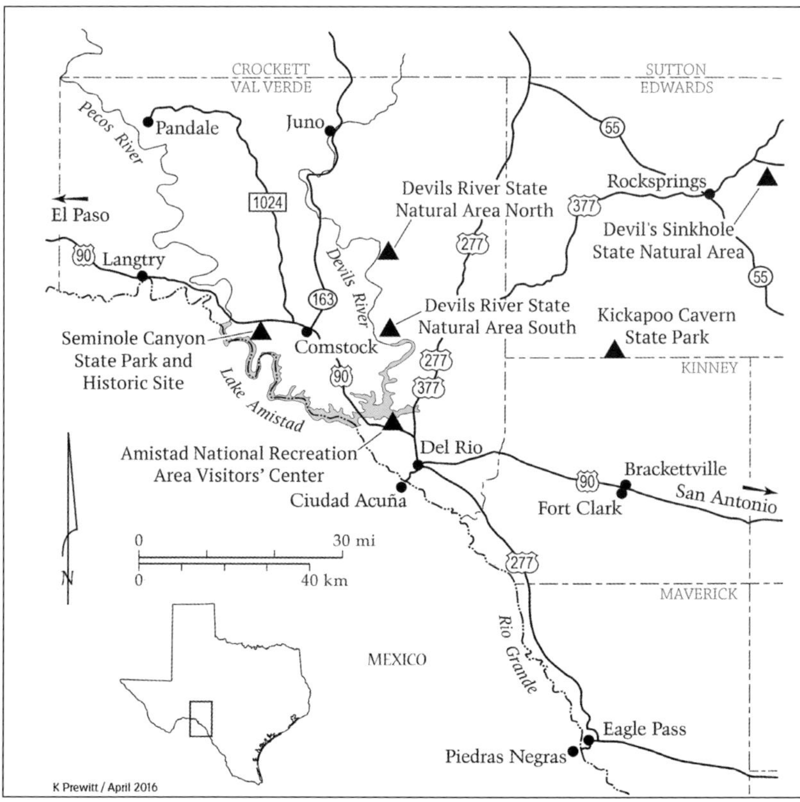

The Lower Pecos Canyonlands

in many places as the only crust of earth. The few trees are stunted. Tall spikes of yucca and sotol spear the sky in spring. Cactus, lechugilla, and Chihuahuan scrub hold on to almost bare stone. Jagged canyons plunge toward river bottoms, often surprising travelers. As the mountains of Mexico loom blue and purple in the southwest, the traveler can sometimes see rain clouds pouring out their gift hundreds of miles away. The sun sets as an orange ball, and the Milky Way dances almost every night. If you luck out and get there after an infrequent rain, the landscape can be transformed. Purple sage billows like the ocean. Ephemeral wild flowers rejoice in every color. Dry creeks run with water. It's a magical place.

Late fall through May are the best times to visit the Lower Pecos Canyonlands. Summers are extremely hot, which can limit many outdoor activities. Winters are generally mild with few really cold days. Many people like to camp, hike the canyons, or fish and hunt the Lower Pecos during the cooler seasons. Places of interest are open year-round, however, for visitors any time of year.

Filling up on gas and buying other essentials in Del Rio, the largest city in the area, is recommended, especially before heading west.

People have left their mark on the landscape for thousands of years. Photo by author.

The Lower Pecos Canyonlands is more or less centered in Val Verde County. Rough boundaries extend west from the Devils River about 100 miles through the Chihuahuan Desert. The southwestern boundaries of the region lie in central Mexico, with the northern boundary perhaps 30 miles north of Del Rio, the major city of the region. Del Rio is about four hours by car from Austin or a little less than three hours from San Antonio. West from Del Rio travelers can reach Big Bend National Park in about four hours.

The towering limestone cliffs formed by the down-cutting river are dotted with shallow overhangs the ranchers call "caves," although most are what archaeologists call rock-shelters (being wider than they are deep). The rock-shelters and caves along the lower part of the Pecos River are also present along the Rio Grande and the Devils River. These natural shelters were used by Native American people for over 10,000 years. These hunter-gatherers lived by gathering plants, hunting animals large and very small, and fishing.

Human beings migrated into the area at the end of the last Ice Age, according to archaeologists. Ancient bones of the now extinct *bison antiquus* have been found in the bottom of a narrow box canyon near Langtry, along with the stone tools ancient hunters used to kill them. About 4,000 years ago they painted numerous stories of their gods on the walls of rockshelters in the canyons. See more information in the chapter on rock art.

Sometime after the Spanish conquest of Mexico in 1521, indigenous North American groups such as Comanches and Apaches moved into the area with their great horse cultures. Even though the horse people were migratory and often rode long distances, they commanded the Lower Pecos Canyonlands for centuries. It was not until the 1880s that Mexican and American settlers, and others, came to the area to raise cattle and build railroads.

The unique history and natural environment of the Lower Pecos Canyonlands make this an interesting place to visit. Over one million visitors come annually to boat and fish at Lake Amistad near Del Rio. Kayakers often stop at the Devils River State Natural Area to put in or take out. Rock art enthusiasts come from all over the world to study the amazing polychrome panels left by the ancients, the most accessible of which are located at Seminole Canyon State Park and Historic Site and the Galloway White Shaman Preserve. Railroad buffs watch long freight trains snake through the rugged terrain near the place where the Silver Spike connected the first southern transcontinental train route in 1883. People interested in the history of the Old West enjoy visiting Langtry, population 14, to see the original Judge Roy Bean saloon, ruins of original settlers' homes, and a wonderful botanical garden focused on plants of the Chihuahuan Desert. Other visitors admire the remains of Fort Clark, where Buffalo Soldiers and others were stationed after the US Civil War. Swimmers delight in the crystal-clear spring-fed pool also at Fort Clark. At night visitors flock to see millions of Mexican free-tailed bats fly from Devil's Sinkhole and Kickapoo Caverns. Those feeling lucky come to gamble in Eagle Pass at the only casino in Texas.

Recommended Highlights

With so much to see and do in Southwest Texas, one trip is not enough. Many people come to the area for specific purposes, like floating the Frio River at Garner State Park or seeing the prehistoric murals at Seminole Canyon State Park and Historic Site. No matter your purpose or final destination, here are some of the top things to do and see as well as places where you can eat and stay in this part of Texas.

1. **Seminole Canyon State Park:** Hike through Seminole Canyon to see 4,000-year-old art left by ancient inhabitants. See the exhibition on local history at the visitor center to learn about prehistoric people, ranching, and the coming of the railroad.
2. **Galloway White Shaman Preserve:** Take the guided tour to this amazing rock art site. Clap your hands in the shelter to hear the echo and contemplate the ancient rituals that may have taken place here.
3. **Langtry:** Visit this ghost town to see Judge Roy Bean's original saloon, crumbling ruins, and a botanical garden with Chihuahuan Desert plants.

Ocotillo blooms in the Chihuahuan Desert. Photo by Thomas C. Self.

4. **Garner State Park:** Float the river and enjoy the cool shade of giant cypresses. Hike to Old Baldy for great views of the Frio canyon. Every summer night you can dance the night away on the patio for free. The old jukebox plays lots of old-time favorites for all ages.
5. **Lost Maples State Park:** Hike through brilliant autumn leaves of bigtooth maples and sycamores along the headwaters of the Sabinal River.
6. **Fort Clark:** Explore this relatively well-preserved US Army fort from 1852. Go to the fort museum to learn the history of the Buffalo Soldiers and Black Seminole Indian scouts.
7. **Las Moras Springs Swimming Pool:** Swim in fresh, cool spring water while at Fort Clark. One of the top three spring-fed pools in Texas. When it's hot, there is nothing better!

Las Moras Springs pool beckons from Fort Clark in Brackettville.
Photo by Thomas C. Self.

8. **Kickapoo Lucky Eagle Casino:** Win some dough at the only casino in Texas.
9. **Laurel Tree Restaurant:** Reserve your table early at this French restaurant in Utopia run by a gourmet chef.
10. **Historic Rocksprings Hotel:** Spend the night here to soak up the atmosphere provided by carefully chosen antiques in all the rooms and a few mounted hunting trophies that pay homage to the great hunting in this area.

Things to Do

Camping and Hiking

Camp under the stars in your tent or RV at Garner State Park, Lost Maples State Natural Area, Seminole Canyon State Park, Kickapoo Caverns State Park, Fort Clark Springs, or along Lake Amistad. Many people bring their RVs to the Del Rio area for the winter season.

Kayaking, Canoeing, and Tubing

You're never far from someplace to get in the water in the Western Hill Country. Bring your kayak or canoe or rent one from a local outfitter. Thousands come just to float down the river in a plastic tube. If you're trying to relax, tubing can't be beat! Experienced kayakers can tackle the float down the Devils River or even the Pecos, but only after good preparation.

Bird-Watching

The Audubon Society rates this area as one of the best bird-watching areas in the United States. This area is the nesting place of the rare golden-cheeked warbler. Golden-cheeked warblers nest only in the mixed Ashe juniper and oak woodlands of Central Texas. They nest from March to July and spend the winter in Mexico and Central America. Warblers eat insects and spiders from oaks and use long strips of cedar bark and spider webs to build nests, where they lay three to four eggs. Loss of nesting habitat has reduced golden-cheeked warbler populations. Black-capped vireos also nest in Texas in the spring (April to July) and spend the winter on the west coast of Mexico. These tiny birds nest in low-growing shrubs and return each year to the same nesting area. Males sing to attract mates and to defend two- to four-acre territories. The loss of low-growing shrub habitat due to grazing, clearing, and fire suppression has led to this bird's endangered status.

Wild Flower and Tree Viewing

Over 300 species of wild flowers abound in the area, such as purple coneflower. Flowers are most abundant during April. Bigtooth maples and sycamores glow with brilliant fall color near Vanderpool in autumn. Follow any road your heart desires to see beautiful colors in spring or fall. Look for hills of purple cenizo after a rain in the desert country.

Visitors often see exotic wildlife on ranches in Southwest Texas. Photo by Thomas C. Self.

Wildlife Viewing

Watch for white-tailed and axis deer, turkeys, giraffes, and other exotics along any road you travel in the Western Hill Country. Seriously. In addition, get reservations for an evening tour to see the bats near Concan or at Devil's Sinkhole State Natural Area or Kickapoo Caverns State Park.

Fishing and Hunting

Some of the best hunting and fishing in the nation is in Southwest Texas. In addition to Lake Amistad, which is well-known for bass fishing, the Nueces River also has largemouth bass, smallmouth bass, and native Guadalupe bass, along with a variety of pan fish such as redbreast sunfish, rock bass, green sunfish, and Rio Grande perch. The American alligator is also abundant in the Nueces River. In the Frio you can see channel catfish, largemouth bass, and a variety of perch in water so crystal-clear that you can actually see the fish you're angling for. Try fly-fishing on the Frio River, too. Rainbow trout are released in the Frio River around January every year. Fishing or hunting licenses are required for everyone over seventeen. Buy one at any fishing/hunting outfitter, at state parks, or online at www.tpwd.texas.gov/business/licenses/online_sales.

Visiting Museums and Historic Forts

From a museum for motorcycles in Vanderpool to one for vice-presidential papers in Uvalde, various museums dot Southwest Texas. Don't forget the exhibit on the Cuban Missile Crisis in Del Rio! Three historic forts in Brackettville, Eagle Pass, and Uvalde provide a glimpse of frontier life.

Viewing Art

The ancient rock art west of Del Rio will amaze you and maybe shake your world. Traditional European and American paintings can be seen for free in Uvalde.

When to Go

Weather is generally good in Southwest Texas, which has hot summers and mild winters. Sunshine predominates with about 227 bright, sunny days each year. Rain is generally sparse in this semiarid continental climate, with an average of about 23 inches per year. Humidity can be high in the summer, however, especially in the eastern counties, due to southeasterly wind from the Gulf of Mexico. Constantly blowing wind can be fierce in some places in winter and spring. High temperatures hover around 100 degrees F in summer, with occasional freezes in winter. Periods of cold weather rarely last more than a few days, and snow is rare. All this being said, I've been there in winter when it was 95 degrees and in March when it snowed.

Rain is the trickiest bit. Mostly it's dry. The rain that does occur usually falls from April through October. But it is not uncommon for tropical weather disturbances and hurricanes to stall out somewhere over Southwest Texas, causing devastating flash floods. The best advice is to watch the weather and be aware. Flash floods roar through canyons with no warning and quickly make roads impassible throughout the area.

This area has many low-water crossings, which means the road crosses ephemeral streams with no bridge. When rains come, water rushes over the road, sometimes with tragic results for drivers and riders. I once drove down Ranch Road 334 south of Camp Wood toward Brackettville and all the low-water crossings were bone dry—except for the one that was running hard with over 10 inches of water. The car wouldn't make it, so I turned around. That cost me another hour and a half on the road. But I got

Swift water can wash vehicles off the road after a strong rain. Photo by author.

where I was going, which is the moral of this story. I got there. There's a local saying in Texas, "Turn around, don't drown." Please take it seriously.

Essentials to Pack

No matter when you go, you will need a hat, preferably one that ties on so it doesn't blow off in the wind or float away down the river. Sunscreen is also a must any time of year. Depending on your activities, you may also need a swimsuit, river shoes, hiking boots, and a hiking stick. Don't forget your camera and, of course, the charger and cord. Also carry drinking water with you, especially in the Chihuahuan Desert.

Seminole Canyon embraces visitors within its stone walls. Photo by author.

Using This Guide

This guide assumes travelers will be driving or riding a motorcycle or a road bike, as other transportation options are extremely limited, although you will occasionally see riders on horseback.

In addition to the modern attractions, this guide also tells about what was once here but no longer hums with daily life. The chapter on rock art describes what was made so long ago and what you can still see. There are also many ghost towns along the way, which make these areas unique. There is even a ghost town underwater!

The chapter on the natural environment details the contrasting geography, flora, and fauna of each subregion. State parks and other public recreation areas are discussed in a chapter, and towns and ghost towns are also detailed. A chapter on historic forts gives information on the remains of US Army forts along the border from 1849. Hunting enthusiasts will find selected outfitters and hunting ranches in a specific chapter to make information easy to find. A unique feature of this guide is the chapter on scenic routes. Finally, the guide ends with a list of movies either filmed in or about the region for your pre- or post-trip perusal.

Information on food and lodging is included at the end of each town's listing. Southwest Texas shares several cultural traits with Mexico, among them being relaxed restaurant service. Service in restaurants is supposed to give you time to relax and enjoy talking to each other. This is not Houston, so relax and enjoy! Restaurants in small towns also tend to be closed on Sunday or at least close earlier than usual, so be prepared.

Stops that welcome groups of motorcycle riders are noted as well as repair shops. I recommend reservations for cabins or campsites during the summer, as places fill up quickly. Also some businesses catering to summer visitors close after the season, so always call ahead for a place to stay.

For those who want more information than this guide can provide, selected references are included at the end. Last you'll find the Tricky Travel Trivia quiz at the end of the book if you're feeling lucky as you drive.

Getting There

The easiest way to travel around Southwest Texas is by car. No commercial airline flights are available directly to Del Rio, Eagle Pass, or Uvalde. The closest general airport is San Antonio, and from there you can rent a car or come by bus.

Bus transportation is available from San Antonio to Uvalde, Eagle Pass, and Del Rio for about $10.00 each way. Once you reach one of these three cities, however, you will still have to rent a car to get to places of interest. Make reservations for both bus and rental car ahead of time to get a seat. Sometimes rental agencies run out of cars.

Greyhound Bus Stations

www.greyhound.com

SAN ANTONIO

500 N. St. Marys St.
210–270–5868

UVALDE

Stripes Valero
2815 US 90
830–278–3458

DEL RIO

Stripes Valero
1602 Veterans Blvd. (US 90)
830–774–5604

EAGLE PASS

Stripes Valero
2013 N. Veteran's Blvd.
830–773–0941

Car Rental Agencies

UVALDE

Enterprise Rent-A-Car
2418 E. Main St.
830–591–0368

Hertz Rent-A-Car
301 Sul Ross Dr.
830–278–1588

Expo Rent-A-Car
2036 Main St.
830–279–0380

DEL RIO

Enterprise Rent-A-Car
2104 Veterans Blvd. (US 90)
830–774–2527

Hertz Rent-A-Car
1104 W. 10th Street
830–778–1085

B&W Auto Rentals
1002 Avenue G
830–775–1658

EAGLE PASS

Enterprise Rent-A-Car
1930 Veteran's Blvd.
830–773–3931

Hertz Rent-A-Car
2033 Veteran's Blvd.
830–757–4271

2

Natural Environment

Southwest Texas presents great variety in landscape as it slopes down from the Edwards Plateau, a large geologic uplift in Central Texas. Rugged limestone canyons and bluffs enclose rivers fed by a large aquifer under the plateau. Large cypress trees sink their knobby roots into the waters of the Western Hill Country, but further west, few trees of any kind remain as the land transitions to the dry Chihuahuan Desert.

The Western Hill Country

Rushing rivers formed the photogenic canyons and valleys of the Western Hill Country over many thousands of years. Water wore away at the porous limestone to form soaring cliffs and gentle curves that enchant all who see them today. Three rivers and their tributaries flow through this region: the Frio, the Nueces, and the Sabinal.

Frio River

Headwaters: The West Frio River rises from springs in northeastern Real County and joins with the East Frio River near the town of Leakey; the Dry Frio River joins northeast of Uvalde.
Mouth: empties into the Nueces River near the town of Three Rivers on the Gulf Coastal Plains
Length: 200 miles
Pro-tip: Riverbanks are privately owned unless in state parks. All persons over seventeen who want to fish must have a license.

Clear rivers with limestone bottoms flow through Southwest Texas. Photo by Thomas C. Self.

The Frio is home to many recreational opportunities in the region. Thousands of people come in the summer to tube, swim, kayak, or canoe the sparkling stream. If you've never done it before, you're in for a treat. Even if you've been tubing a hundred times in other places, you'll find that the Frio is one of the best. Plan a half-day trip, minimum, depending on how fast the water is flowing. Outfitters can tell you about how long a particular trip will last. Many resorts and cabins as well as Garner State Park have Frio River frontage and access. See more in the chapter on state parks.

History

Alonso De León called this waterway the Rio Sarco in 1689, but "Frio" is what stuck. *Frio* is Spanish for "cold." Leaving the Western Hill County, the Frio is dammed to form Choke Canyon Lake near the town of Three Rivers before joining the Nueces on its way to the Gulf. Even today the Frio is "out in the middle of nowhere, most cell phones don't work and it is not near a Wal-Mart or McDonalds. And those are just a few of the good parts," to quote a character called "Texas Bob." The best part is that the Frio offers 47 miles of cold, clear water suitable for tubing and kayaking among high limestone bluffs, boulders, and enormous cypress trees.

You should be aware that the Frio goes "on a rise" occasionally after a heavy rain and can become dangerous. Always check weather and rain conditions before getting into any river. Get out of the water if a storm comes up. Being struck by lightning pretty much ends the party. Accessing the

Huge cypress trees line areas of deep water on the Frio.
Photo by Thomas C. Self.

riverbanks is legal only when portaging canoes or scouting for obstructions.

For information on camping and lodging near the Frio, see Concan in the chapter on towns, and see Garner State Park in the chapter on state parks.

Nueces River

Headwaters: Edwards Plateau, approximately 50 miles north of Uvalde
Mouth: empties in the Gulf of Mexico at Corpus Christi Bay
Length: 315 miles
Pro-tip: All persons over seventeen who want to fish must have a license. Do not cross a fence to get to the river, as the banks are all private property. The river itself is public access, however.

The beautiful, crystal-clear water of the Nueces River flows through the limestone bluffs of the Edwards Plateau as the river winds its way downstream all the way to the Gulf of Mexico. Fed by springs in the Western Hill Country, the Nueces flows through a canyon of remarkable beauty paralleling Ranch Road 335. Several branches join the river on its way to the Gulf Coast, where it empties in Corpus Christi Bay. Some say it is the "Mother River of the Hill Country" since the Frio and Sabinal Rivers feed into it. Several resorts and cabins have Nueces River frontage and access. See more under Camp

The Nueces River is dammed near Camp Wood for perfect swimming. Photo by Thomas C. Self.

Wood in the chapter on towns. Texas 55 crosses the Nueces several times between Uvalde and Camp Wood. Find a place to pull over near a low-water crossing and jump in!

History

The original Indian name for this river seems to have been Chotilapacquen. The Nueces River first appeared on a European map in 1527, identified as Hidden River. The French explorer René Robert Cavelier, Sieur de La Salle, tried to sail to this river in 1685, believing that it was the Mississippi from his poorly marked map. Four years later, in 1689, the Spaniard Alonso De León was sent from Mexico to find La Salle's settlement (which was on the Gulf Coast) and crossed the Nueces. He named it Río de las Nueces, or River of Nuts, for the pecan trees growing along its banks. The Spanish established several short-lived missions on the Nueces in 1762. The Nueces was the boundary line between the Spanish provinces of Texas and Nuevo Santander.

The Battle of the Nueces

A Civil War skirmish known as the battle of the Nueces took place on the morning of August 10, 1862, when mounted Confederate soldiers attacked a force of Hill Country Unionists, encamped en route to Mexico on the west bank of the Nueces River about 20 miles from Fort Clark in present-day Kinney County. The Unionists, mostly German settlers from Fredericksburg, had camped without choosing a defensive position or posting a strong guard. The ninety-four Confederates, led by Lt. C. D. McRae, came upon the camp on the afternoon of August 9. Firing began an hour before sunlight the next morning; ten of the sixty-one to sixty-eight Unionists were killed, and nine were wounded. The nine wounded were executed a few hours after the battle. Two Confederates were killed and eighteen wounded, including McRae. Of the Unionists who escaped from the battle, eight were killed by Confederates on October 18, 1862, while trying to cross into Mexico, eleven reached home, and most of the others escaped temporarily to Mexico or to California. Some of the survivors, who included John W. Sansom and German members of the Union League from the area around Comfort, organized a militia to protect parts of Kendall, Gillespie, and Kerr Counties from Indian raids and Confederate actions and eventually joined Unionist forces headquartered in New Orleans. A monument was erected in Comfort in 1866, the only German-language monument to the Union in the South.

For ten years—from the Texas Revolution in 1836 to the end of the Mexican War in 1846—Mexico claimed the Nueces as the boundary with Texas rather than the more southerly Rio Grande. The Treaty of Guadalupe Hidalgo in 1846 settled the matter at its present line on the Rio Grande.

Sabinal River

Headwaters: Lost Maples State Natural Area
Mouth: empties into the Frio River about 10 miles south of the town of Sabinal
Length: 60 miles
Pro-tip: Most property along the Sabinal is private with few public access points.

History

The third river in the Western Hill County is the short Sabinal River. A Comanche trail once followed its course and was marked on early Spanish maps. The sparkling stream was originally called Arroyo de la Soledad by the Spanish, meaning "Stream of Solitude." The river traverses flat to rolling terrain with fractures, faults, and folds, surfaced by sandy and clay loam that supports hardwoods and grasses. In several places the river sinks underground to rise again downstream. The Sabinal River is quite shallow, making it unsuitable for tubing or kayaking.

The Sabinal River starts from springs in Lost Maples State Natural Area. Photo by Thomas C. Self.

The canyons of the Lower Pecos present breathtaking views along the rivers.
Photo by Thomas C. Self.

The Lower Pecos Canyonlands

The Lower Pecos Canyonlands lie in the vast Chihuahuan Desert. Everything from El Paso to Del Rio is in this desert. In addition, the Chihuahuan Desert is home to Big Bend National Park, Guadalupe Mountains National Park, and the Davis Mountains.

The presence of water brought people to the Lower Pecos Canyonlands long ago and keeps them here today. As late as the 1880s, there were many springs in this area, from which crystal-clear water flowed. Most of the springs are dry now due to increased population and grazing, but some still feed the rivers and lakes of the area.

Chihuahuan Desert

Size: more than 200,000 square miles, mostly in Mexico

Average annual rainfall in Del Rio: about 20 inches

Average high in July/August: 97 degrees F

Average low in January: 64 degrees F

Pro-tip: Carry water with you at all times. Sunscreen is a must. Wear a wide-brimmed hat that ties on because the winds and the sun can be fierce.

Sotol spears the sky in the rugged Chihuahuan Desert. Photo by Thomas C. Self.

The Chihuahuan is not the red-orange desert of western movies but instead is more subtle and diverse. The colors are soft, the plants sparse, and the rocks plentiful. Many birds and animals are here year-round and many more migrate through. Contrary to what you may have heard, however, packs of Chihuahuas do not roam the desert yapping at the moon. The dog we know as the Chihuahua may indeed have originated in the state of Chihuahua, Mexico, several thousand years ago.

Ecology

Del Rio lies on the eastern edge of the great Chihuahuan Desert, which covers all of Texas west of the Pecos River. The desert spreads into New Mexico and a bit of Arizona and dips down deep into central Mexico.

The Chihuahuan Desert is special for many reasons. The region is one of the most biologically diverse arid regions in the world and supports more cacti than any other place on earth. Some botanists think perhaps all cacti originated here and spread to other regions of the world from the Lower Pecos. Of the more than 500 types of cacti in the region, prickly pears, hedgehogs, living rocks, nipple cacti, and cory cacti are most prevalent.

Stem succulents such as lechuguilla, sotol, and various types of yuccas characterize the Chihuahuan Desert scrub. Other common shrubs include mimosa, acacia, mesquite, mariola, fourwing saltbush, tarbush, javelinabush, skeletonleaf goldeneye, allthorn, and ocotillo. The short, stubby lechugilla agave is one of the defining plants of the Chihuahuan Desert. No lechugilla, no Chihuahua.

The low-growing lechugilla is a distinctive plant of the Chihuahuan Desert. Photo by author.

The desert also provides nesting sites and migratory habitats for more than 500 bird species. In the desert scrub roadrunners scurry after earless lizards while golden eagles search among the agave and creosote for black-tailed jackrabbits. In addition, over 110 native species of freshwater fish swim in the desert rivers.

The Chihuahuan Desert is home to a multitude of specialized insects. Among them are the desert tarantula, whip scorpion or vinegarroon, desert millipede, and giant centipede. Many butterflies and moths are also found here. If you are lucky, perhaps you will see monarch butterflies on their annual migration to overwinter in Mexico.

A great number of lizards inhabit the region. Among these are the whiptails, spinys, horned, collared, and geckos. Snakes have evolved to take advantage of a wide range of conditions. While a few are diurnal—such as the garter snake and coachwhip—most avoid the heat of the sun by prowling after dark. Chihuahuan snake species include the beautiful Mexican king snake, Trans-Pecos rat snake, and many species of rattlesnakes.

Mammals are diverse and tend to be nocturnal. The northern Chihuahuan Desert has one of the richest bat faunas to be found anywhere. Eighteen species have been documented in Presidio County alone. Most are small and insectivorous. Notable representatives include the pallid bat, western pipistrelle, and Brazilian free-tailed bat. Millions of Mexican free-tailed bats fly out from Kickapoo Caverns State Park or Devil's Sinkhole State Natural Area every evening in warm months.

Mule deer, white-tailed deer, and pronghorn are common residents. Desert bighorn sheep have been successfully reintroduced to many of the desert mountain ranges in the northern Chihuahuan Desert. Other common mammals include the coyote, collared peccary (or javelina), ringtail, black-tailed jackrabbit, spotted ground squirrel, a number of skunk species, wood rats, and many nocturnal mice. The larger predators have struggled for survival, but mountain lions still occur here, and black bears are making a return to the northern Chihuahuan Desert region. Grizzly bears were found in at least one Chihuahuan Desert mountain range until the late 1960s.

Great places to visit the desert are at Seminole Canyon State Park and Judge Roy Bean Visitor Center and Botanical Garden in Langtry, maintained by the Texas Highway Department. See information for Langtry in the chapter on ghost towns. For more specific information on what to see and do in the area, see the chapters on state parks and towns.

Amistad Reservoir

US 90, west of Del Rio

Total shoreline: 851 miles; 547 miles are in the United States, and 304 miles are in Mexico (compared with the entire Texas coastline of 367 miles). The Rio Grande arm extends up the river 78 miles; the Pecos River arm extends up the river 14 miles; the Devils River arm extends up the river 25 miles.

Lake Amistad is a great place for bass fishing. Photo by Stephen L. Black.

Size: 5,568,500 acre-feet; the second-largest lake in Texas after Toledo Bend Reservoir

Cost: $125 million (1969 dollars) to build; the United States' share was 56.2 percent; Mexico's share was 43.8 percent.

Evaporation: At 100 degrees F, 3,000 acre-feet or 131,000,000 gallons/day evaporate from Amistad Reservoir.

History and Ecology

Lake Amistad is a reservoir on the Rio Grande at its confluence with the Devils River. The lake is bounded by Val Verde County on the Texas side of the international border and the state of Coahuila on the Mexican side of the border. The reservoir was formed in November 1969 by the construction of Amistad Dam to provide flood control, water conservation, irrigation, hydroelectric power, and recreation to the area. The dam and lake are managed jointly by the governments of the United States and Mexico through the International Boundary and Water Commission, which was established in 1889 to maintain the border, allocate river waters between the two nations, and provide for flood control and water sanitation. *Amistad* is the Spanish word for "friendship." The lake is known in Spanish as Presa Amistad.

Rated by ESPN as the top bass lake in America, Amistad Reservoir is stocked with fish, including largemouth and smallmouth bass, Guadalupe bass, and catfish. Records include a largemouth bass over 15 pounds, a channel catfish over 14 pounds, and the whopper, a striped bass weighing

Purple cenizo blooms near Lake Amistad after a good rain. Photo by Jack Johnson.

in at 45 pounds! You can see why fishing tournaments attract sportsmen from all over to this lake. There is usually at least one tournament going on at any time during the year.

Amistad National Recreation Area supports flora and fauna in a combination not found in any other National Park Service site. This biodiversity is a result of the park's location in a transition zone between three major plant communities: Tamaulipan Shrubland, Chihuahuan Desert, and Edwards Plateau. This mix of habitats is combined with a huge expanse of the clear, clean waters of Amistad Reservoir. One species of native fish, *Amistad gambusia*, did not survive the inundation of its habitat at Goodenough Springs, however, which is now under 70 feet of water since the construction of the dam. The fish became extinct by 1987.

In the fall thousands of monarch butterflies roost on park lands before continuing their journey south to wintering sites in Mexico. Many waterfowl species spend the winter on the lake before returning north in the spring. Even endangered and threatened species, such as the interior least tern, use the lake to nest and raise young.

For details on boating, fishing, and camping at Lake Amistad, see the chapter on state parks. Lodging options for Lake Amistad can be found with Del Rio in the chapter on towns.

Las Moras Springs and Creek

US 90, Brackettville
Headwaters: on the grounds of Fort Clark
Mouth: empties into the Rio Grande
Public access: at Fort Clark

The pool at Fort Clark is the third-largest spring-fed pool in Texas. Photo by Thomas C. Self.

Las Moras Springs, located at Fort Clark in Brackettville, are one of the many that drew people here as long as 10,000 years ago and continue to attract visitors today. The crystal-clear water at the Fort Clark Springs pool, the third-largest spring-fed swimming pool in Texas, is about 72 degrees year-round. You can get a day pass that entitles you to swimming, 21 miles of hike and bike trails, a nine-hole par 3 golf course, and other amenities. For more information, see the entry for Brackettville in the Towns chapter.

Devils River

Length: 94 miles
Headwaters: Edwards Plateau in Sutton County
Mouth: empties into Lake Amistad
Public access: very limited

Ecology

The Devils River flows through remote, rugged country through Southwest Texas. Fresh springs trickle clean water into the river in many places along its route to Lake Amistad, especially around Dolan Falls. The river also runs underground for about 20 miles near Juno, where sand and gravel filter the water before it reemerges. Because of its pristine quality and unique natural environment, the river is protected by the Nature Conservancy, the Texas Parks and Wildlife Department, and private ranch owners along the entire route. The best way to enjoy the river is to visit the Devils River State Natural Area, located off TX 277.

The Devils River is one of the most pristine streams in North America. Photo by Jack Johnson.

The riparian corridor nurtures many rare and endangered species, including the almost extinct Texas snowbell (*Styrax platanifolius* subsp. *texanus),* a small tree with white flowers in spring. The snowbell grows in limestone crevices near rivers or springs. There are only ten groups of these trees known today, all in Texas. The endangered black-capped vireo returns every spring to nest along the Devils River, and monarch butterflies fly above the river as they migrate each year. Bats come to Fern Cave, an 80-foot sinkhole, to have their babies each year from May to October.

Pecos River

Length: 926 miles
Headwaters: Sangre de Cristo Mountains near Pecos, New Mexico
Mouth: empties into the Rio Grande
Public access: very limited

History and Ecology

The river is named for Native Americans who lived at Pecos Pueblo about AD 800 in what is today New Mexico. The first European to cross the river was conquistador Francisco Vásquez de Coronado, who reached the area in 1541. Gaspar Castaño de Sosa, who followed the Pecos northward, called it the Río Salado because of its salty taste, which caused it to be shunned by men and animals alike. The earliest European settlement was founded in 1794 at San Miguel del Bado in the upper valley of the Pecos. With the Anglo-American occupation of Texas, the middle and upper valley became the chief western cattle trail to the north as well as the site of several famous cattle ranches.

Travelers can view the stone canyon of the Pecos River at the bridge over US 90. Photo by Thomas C. Self.

Fort Lancaster, in present-day Crockett County, was built near the river in 1855. Except for settlement around the fort, the earliest Anglo settlement in Texas on the river was the town of Pecos, founded in 1881 when the Texas and Pacific Railway crossed West Texas. Early-day travelers described the river as generally 65 to 100 feet wide and 7 to 10 feet deep, with a fast current.

Irrigation from the Red Bluff Reservoir in West Texas has greatly reduced the flow of water in the river since the 1930s. Since 1969, Amistad Reservoir has also affected water flow.

The topography of the river valley ranges from mountain pastures in New Mexico, with an elevation of more than 13,000 feet above sea level, to grasslands, semiarid irrigated farmlands, desert with sparse vegetation, and, in the lowermost reaches of the river, deep canyons. The Pecos serves as the eastern boundary of the most mountainous and arid region of Texas, generally known as the Trans-Pecos. From below Sheffield in eastern Pecos County to the river's confluence with the Rio Grande, the river passes through a deep gorge, a natural barrier to river access.

For a sweeping vista of the river and canyon, stop at the Pecos River Overlook on US 90 about 40 miles west of Del Rio. You can also take the scenic route to Pandale, where you can swim, boat, and fish in the river. More information is found in the chapter on scenic routes.

Rio Grande

Length: almost 2,000 miles (estimates vary as the riverbed changes course)
Headwaters: San Juan Mountains, near Creede, Colorado
Mouth: empties into the Gulf of Mexico
Public access: limited access near Del Rio

History and Ecology

The "Big River" or Rio Grande forms the border between the United States and Mexico in Texas. Originating as a snow-fed mountain spring near the Continental Divide in the San Juan Mountains of Colorado, the river flows almost 2,000 miles. Depending on how it is measured, the Rio Grande is the twenty-second-longest river in the world and the fourth- or fifth-longest in North America.

The river runs through forests 12,000 feet high in the mountains, through long stretches of the Chihuahuan Desert and the Tamilipan scrub, to citrus

Brush chokes the Rio Grande in some parts of southwest Texas. Photo by Jack Johnson.

orchards near McAllen, and finally to the Gulf of Mexico. Water quantity and quality vary greatly along the way—from clear mountain stream to almost dry around El Paso to relatively clean near Del Rio to muddy and garbage-filled in other parts.

Native Americans undoubtedly used the river for drinking and transportation, but the first Europeans to explore it were Spanish conquistadors. It is believed that Alvar Nuñez Cabeza de Vaca crossed the Rio Grande in 1535, and Francisco Vásquez de Coronado in 1540. Juan de Oñate is believed to have been the first to call the river the Rio Grande when he crossed it near today's El Paso.

The first person to document the 190-mile "wild and scenic" section from Big Bend National Park to Langtry was geologist Robert Hill in 1899. Because of the river's many twists and turns, and various demands for water usage, the exact boundary between Mexico and the United States has been disputed many times. Currently the river is closely patrolled on the US side by the US Border Patrol.

Many people have made the fifteen-minute swim across the river, but if you start on the US side, it is illegal to touch the Mexican side, according to treaty. There are strong undercurrents in many places, and swimming is not recommended. Please cross only at designated border crossings.

Good places to see the river include the International Bridge between Del Rio and Ciudad Acuña or the Amistad Dam International Crossing off Spur 349 off US 90 west of Del Rio. See the chapters on towns and state parks for details.

The serene San Felipe Creek flows through Del Rio. Photo by Thomas C. Self.

San Felipe Springs and Creek

US 90 East, Del Rio, near RR 2523

Length: 9 miles

Headwaters: about 3 miles northeast of downtown Del Rio

Mouth: empties into the Rio Grande

Public access: Del Rio city parks

History and Ecology

Early explorers described seven deep, clear pools at San Felipe Springs, with many large fish, surrounded by hackberry trees, grapevines, and cattails. Gaspar Castaño de Sosa may have been the first European to visit in 1590. By the late seventeenth century many other Spanish explorers and settlers had become familiar with the springs since the Kings Highway (Camino Real) to San Antonio and El Paso passed right by.

Between 1672 and 1783 several attempts by the Spanish government of New Spain to establish settlements in the area were unsuccessful. By the mid-1800s, mounted cavalry units and stagecoaches were making great use of the springs. James and Paula Taylor established the first permanent settlement in 1862, and development along the creek was rapid. Irrigation canals and dams were built to water vineyards, orchards, and gardens, and springwater was hauled and sold in town until 1900, when a city water system was installed. In 1882 two gristmills were using the water for power, and by 1901 there was also an electric light and ice plant.

San Felipe Springs is the fourth-largest spring in Texas in terms of water discharge. There are ten separate springs that form the creek. Springs 2 and 3 provide drinking water to the city of Del Rio and Laughlin Air Force Base. Threatened and endangered species along San Felipe Creek include the black-capped vireo, least tern, mountain plover, Texas hornshell mussel, Texas snowbell, Tobusch fishook cactus, and Devils River minnow.

Looking across the Chihuahuan Desert toward the mountains of Mexico. Photo by Thomas C. Self.

3

State Parks and Other Public Recreation Areas

Due to the unique location, Southwest Texas has some of the most diverse parkland in the country. From kayaking in a river to spelunking in an underground cave, you are never far from adventure. Visitors can get close to nature, whether in the woods or in the desert. Bring your fishing rod, camera, and hiking boots, and let's go!

Amistad National Recreation Area

4121 Veterans Blvd. (US 90 W) (headquarters, bookstore, and museum)
Del Rio, TX 78840
830–775–7491
www.nps.gov/amis
Hours: Tuesday–Saturday, 8:00 a.m.–4:30 p.m.
Pro-tip: Permits are required for camping and for boating and fishing on the lake. All persons over seventeen who want to fish must have a license.

Stop by the headquarters building to get maps and permits and to visit the excellent bookstore and museum of the area. Eight picnic areas can be found around the lake for picnicking or swimming. Governors Landing has a day use area for picnicking, swimming, and enjoying a walk by the water. Visitors can swim anywhere in the lake except in coves with boat ramps or marinas. At Diablo East the unpaved Viewpoint Road offers sweeping views of the lake and has good spots for picnicking, swimming, and scuba diving.

Lake Amistad offers great swimming, boating, and fishing. Photo by Stephen L. Black.

Tent and RV Camping

Fees: $4.00–$8.00 per night

Reservations: None; first come, first served. Permits are required, however.

Pro-tip: Bring extra tarps and rope to create a shaded picnic table space. Stake your tent down well and put on the rainfly for extra protection. The wind can really blow.

Amistad National Recreation Area's campgrounds are primitive. All sites have covered picnic tables and barbecue grills. There are no hookups, though most sites will accommodate RVs. An RV dump station with potable water is located along the road to the Diablo East boat ramp. The only other potable water is at Governors Landing campsite. Campgrounds are generally open all year. Most campgrounds have volunteer camp hosts during winter months. Pay at each campground; there is a fee station centrally located. Senior Pass and Golden Access holders are entitled to a 50 percent discount. Quiet hours are from 10:00 p.m. to 6:00 a.m. Loud or intrusive noise is prohibited at all times. Numerous commercial RV parks in the Del Rio area offer full services.

Campgrounds in Amistad National Recreation Area

Name	No. of Sites	Fee per Night	Description
Governors Landing	15	$8.00	Suitable for tents and RVs less than 28 feet. The only ANRA campground with potable water available. No hookups.
San Pedro	35	$4.00	Suitable for tents and RVs, but no drinking water or hookups available. There are 5 tent-only sites available. The campground is accessed via a short gravel road.
277 North	17	$4.00	Suitable for tents and RVs, but no drinking water or hookups available.
Spur 406	6	$4.00	Suitable for tents and RVs, but no drinking water or hookups available.
Rough Canyon	4	$4.00	Suitable for tents and RVs, but no drinking water or hookups available.

Amistad National Recreation Area Boat Launch

US 90, about 39 miles west of Del Rio

Look for a brown Amistad National Recreation Area (ANRA) sign pointing left. You will see the collapsed roof of an abandoned service station. Go left on the paved road to a large boat launch and picnic area. There are a number of covered picnic tables with grills and stunning views of the canyon and the conjunction of the Pecos and Rio Grande Rivers. There is plenty of room for boat trailer parking, but swimming is not allowed.

Amistad Dam International Crossing

Spur 349, off US 90 west

Pro-tip: A passport is required to enter Mexico.

Another interesting view of the Rio Grande is from the Amistad Reservoir Dam, built in 1969. There's a small parking lot atop the dam on the US side of the international boundary line. At the foot of the dam the water of the Rio Grande looks cool and green.

Devils River State Natural Area

Off Texas 277, about 65 miles from Del Rio

830–395–2133; 512–389–8901 (campsite reservations)

www.tpwd.texas.gov/state-parks/devils-river

Hours: Friday–Monday, gate open from 8:00 a.m. to 5:00 p.m.

Fees: free day use, $5.00 to $10.00 fee for camping

Reservations: required

Pro-tip: All camping is by reservation only, paid in advance. If there is more than a few inches of water at any low-water crossing over a highway or road, please do not try to cross. Flash floods occur almost every year. Fill up with gas and essentials before you come. The nearest service station is 25 miles away and is not open all the time. The nearest full-service station is 65 miles away.

Devils River State Natural Area offers a great place to kayak or fish. Photo by Jack Johnson.

Devils River State Natural Area is for those wanting a rugged, remote experience. Visitors can enjoy day hiking, primitive camping, nature viewing, mountain biking, horse-back riding, swimming, and guided rock art tours (by appointment only). This is a popular place for kayakers paddling down from Baker's Crossing on the Devils River to camp. Devils River State Natural Area is unique in that it is primitive and isolated, with few amenities. Visitors should bring their own food and water and be prepared for a rugged wilderness experience.

To reach the state natural area from Texas 277, turn left on Dolan Creek Road and go 18.6 miles to the park entrance. Dolan Creek Road is a rough, 22-mile gravel/dirt county road with multiple low-water crossings. Use caution if you see flowing water! This is working ranch country, so please drive carefully and be mindful of loose livestock. High-clearance vehicles with 8-ply rating minimum (to minimize flats and blowouts) are recommended.

The 37,000-acre state natural area consists of two units—the original 20,000-acre state natural area, now called Del Norte, and the newly acquired 17,000-acre unit known as Big Satan, or, more formally, the Dan A. Hughes unit. Only Del Norte was open to the public when this book went to press; check the website for the opening of Big Satan.

Before kayaking or fishing on the Devils River, you are encouraged to visit the website (www.tpwd.texas.gov/state-parks/devils-river/river-trips) and check the river conditions; then contact one of the outfitters listed below. These outfitters are authorized by the Texas Parks and Wildlife Department to provide shuttle and guide services for paddling and fishing trips that launch and/or take out on the Devils River State Natural Area units.

Amistad Expeditions: 512–923–2344; www.amistadexpeditions.com. Shuttle service and river guide service.

Expedition Outfitters: 210–602–9284; www.expeditionoutfitters.net. Guided fly-fishing trips.

Reel Fly: 830–964–4823; www.reelfly.net. Guided fly-fishing trips, shuttle service, and boat rentals.

Devil's Sinkhole State Natural Area

US 377, about 6 miles northeast of Rocksprings
101 N. Sweeten St. on the square (Rocksprings Visitor Center)
Rocksprings, TX 78880
830–663–2287 or 830–563–2342 (Kickapoo Caverns)
www.tpwd.texas.gov/state-parks/devils-sinkhole

Mexican free-tailed bats fly from Devil's Sinkhole to catch insects in the evening. Courtesy Texas Parks and Wildlife Department.

Hours: Wednesday–Sunday, 10:00 a.m.–3:00 p.m., May through October (visitor center)

Reservations: required in advance

Fees: $6.00 to $20.00

Pro-tip: Access is limited to guided tours. Wheelchairs are welcome.

See millions of Mexican free-tailed bats fly out of the Devil's Sinkhole cavern every evening May through October. The cavern is home to over 3 million Mexican free-tailed bats, one of the state's largest colonies. Tours offer the opportunity to watch them fly out as they leave the cave for their nocturnal feeding. These bats consume an estimated 250 tons of insects every night. Evening bat flight tours go throughout the summer, and guided nature hikes are scheduled on the first and third Saturdays of every month except during hunting season. Day tours can be arranged with a minimum of three days' notice. Reservations are required. All tours meet at the visitor center in downtown Rocksprings.

Even though archaeologists have found only sparse cultural remains near the Devil's Sinkhole, it is likely that human beings have been gathering here for over 6,000 years. Certainly native people utilized the high-quality flint found near here for making tools such as knives and scrapers. Because of the unique characteristics of the site, it is highly possible that ancient people would have also considered this a sacred place, a place to connect with the underworld and speak to the gods.

Evidence from other sinkhole sites on the Edwards Plateau and in the Lower Pecos Canyonlands indicates that these features were often used for burial of the dead and played integral roles in the sacred as well as the physical landscape of Native Americans. Sinkholes as well as caves, crevices, springs, and seeps were considered to be avenues to the underworld.

Settlers to this area discovered the cavern in 1867, and cowboys and cavers immediately started exploring the cave and writing their initials on the limestone walls. Twentieth-century entrepreneurs turned to even less prosaic endeavors to mine the sinkhole for bat guano, which was processed into fertilizer.

Located just north of Rocksprings in Edwards County near the headwaters of Hackberry Creek, the sinkhole is a vertical cavern cutting into Edwards Limestone with an opening measuring approximately 40 feet by 60 feet and a vertical drop to the main cavern of about 140 feet. The main cavern is circular and reaches a total depth of 350–400 feet. Part of a vast karst system of underground caves in the porous Edwards Plateau, the sinkhole was created when an underground solution cavity collapsed.

Most of the 1,860 acres of the park is natural and undeveloped, but there are trails for guided hikes and two bird blinds for bird-watching. At the sinkhole you can step out over the chasm onto the wheelchair-accessible viewing platform and peer down into the depths below. To protect this sensitive natural resource, visitors are not allowed to enter the sinkhole itself.

Garner State Park

RR 1050, off US 83, near Concan
830–232–6132
512–389–9000 or https:texas.reserveworld.com (reservations)
www.garnerstatepark.com
Hours: Daily, year-round; office: 8:00 a.m.–10:00 p.m.
Fees: adult day use, $7.00; additional fees for overnight stays
Pro-tip: Make camping reservations well in advance. Dancing on a summer's night is very popular with all ages and is a must-do activity. Don't forget your sunscreen and hat when hiking or floating.

Beautiful cool water beckons at Garner State Park. Photo by Thomas C. Self.

The park is a great family vacation spot for camping, swimming, fishing, and tubing. The park includes concessions, a dance pavilion, restrooms with showers, laundry facilities, and putt-putt golf.

History and Ecology

Between 10,000 and 12,000 years ago, prehistoric people camped on the banks of the Frio. They came here for the abundant game, useful plants, and stone for making tools. Native Americans continuously lived here until the 1850s, when settlers began trickling west of San Antonio. Two German immigrant families, the Magers and the Streibs, settled on land that later became Garner State Park. During the Depression of the 1930s, local citizens acquired the land and enlisted the Civilian Conservation Corps (CCC) to build the park. The CCC utilized native limestone and hewn bald cypress to construct the buildings and dance pavilion. The park opened in 1941 and was named for John Nance Garner, then vice-president of the United States.

The park has almost 3 miles of Frio River frontage, winding through 1,774 acres of scenic Western Hill Country terrain. Deep canyons, crystal-clear streams, high mesas, and carved limestone cliffs characterize this dramatic landscape. Located on the western edge of the Edwards Plateau, Garner State Park is part of a unique sub-region known as the Balcones

Canyonlands. Edwards limestone uplifted millions of years ago, creating steep canyon walls and some of the most spectacular views in the Texas Hill Country.

The rock formations in the park were created in the Cretaceous age, which lasted from 138 million to 63 million years ago. The Glen Rose formation, a collection of limestone, shale, marl, and siltstone beds, arose from sediment along the shifting margins of an ancient sea. Dinosaurs roamed there and left footprints in the sands. The sea then spread over the rest of Texas, depositing the Edwards formation limestone over the Glen Rose beds. This layering of Glen Rose below and Edwards above is found throughout this area.

Park visitors will see white-tailed deer, axis deer, black rock and fox squirrels, raccoons, and many other species. Rio Grande turkeys, mourning doves, black and turkey vultures, eastern bluebirds, and several species of migratory birds reside here. Two endangered species nest in the park: the golden-cheeked warbler and the black-capped vireo.

Water Sports

That's really what it's all about at Garner: swimming, tubing, kayaking, and paddle-boating. Rent tubes, kayaks, and paddle boats at the concession stand. Tube in the park from Bridge Crossing to Magers Crossing. Longer river trips can be made outside the park.

Putt-Putt Golf

Near the Pavilion
Hours: Daily, 10:00 a.m.–10:15 p.m., early March to mid-August; Saturday and Sunday only during the off-season. Closed December through early March.
Fee: $5.00

Dancing

On the Pavilion
Hours: nightly during summer
Fee: free

Every night in the summer, the park's outdoor dance floor is filled with people. A Texas tradition dating back to the 1940s, the dance uses a quarter-fed

Tips for a Successful Tubing Float Trip

- ✔ Wear good water shoes that will not fall off. Some rivers have rock bottoms, and you may need to stand up along your float.
- ✔ Reapply sunscreen throughout your tubing trip. Getting sunburned is no fun.
- ✔ Tie on sunglasses and headwear. Be sure they are attached to something so they do not sink to the bottom. You can buy sunglass strings with floaties on them that you pull over the stems of your glasses to keep them on. The floaties help in case you flip out of your tube. Many a pair of prescription glasses have been lost in the river.
- ✔ Drink water from plastic or metal containers along the way. Bring plenty. Floating in the hot sun can be dehydrating.
- ✔ Do not bring your cell phone or other electronic devices.
- ✔ Waterproof cameras are perfect; just make sure you tie them onto something that will float.
- ✔ Do not take your car keys or room keys on the river. You can buy "safe boxes" to wear around your neck to put valuables in, but I don't guarantee they will float. Waistband zipper pouches are also available.
- ✔ Do not wear or bring jewelry or valuables. Men, this means you too!
- ✔ Outside Garner State Park, the banks of the Frio are privately owned. Do not trespass on private property.
- ✔ Plan to carry out all your trash. Keep the river clean.
- ✔ Do not bring glass or Styrofoam on the river.
- ✔ The Frio River is a family river. Please respect your fellow tubers and be polite.

jukebox that plays popular and timeless country tunes. Line dances are a dance floor favorite. Family friendly. Alcohol is not permitted, but refreshments are available at the Garner Grill.

Hiking

Pro-tip: Please be aware that poison ivy may grow near some trails. Drink plenty of water when engaging in outdoor activities, and use plenty of sunscreen. Lastly, please do not hike alone. It's more fun with a friend!

Hiking Trails at Garner State Park

Name	Length	Time	Difficulty	Description
Old CCC Entrance Road	0.84 mile	20 min.	Easy	Open to hikers and bikers, this paved road is a good place to look for endangered golden-cheeked warblers in spring.
Donovan Trail	0.70 mile	30 min.	Moderate	This trail provides access to some of the best examples of habitats found in the Western Hill Country.
Bridges Trail	0.65 mile	45 min.	Challenging	Loose rocks and steep terrain. A great view of Old Baldy at Painted Rock Overlook and the shade of the giant Ashe juniper tree.
Crystal Cave Trail	0.62 mile	45 min.	Challenging	Challenging trail in several locations; provides access to one of the park's natural wonders.
Blinn River Trail	0.53 mile	20 min.	Easy	Stroll along the Frio River.
Old Baldy Trail	0.53 mile	45 min.	Challenging	A steep, rocky trail that gives a bird's-eye view of the Frio Canyon.
Foshee Trail	1.66 miles	60 min.	Moderate	This trail transects the mountains of Garner State Park. Many trails intersect the Foshee Trail, giving access to most of the backcountry area of the park.
Ashe Juniper Trail	2.49 miles	1.5 hours	Moderate	Vistas of the backside of Old Baldy and access to the Youth Group Camping Area.
Old Horse Trail	0.48 mile	30 min.	Moderate	Narrow old horse trail through the trees, traversing the steep slope of the mountain several hundred feet above the Old Entrance Road.
Frio Canyon Trail	2.88 miles	1.5 hours	Easy	Relatively flat hike-and-bike trail with views of the mountains and canyon around the Frio River.

Eleven miles of trails offer both easy and challenging hikes. Trail maps are available at the office.

Camping

Pro-tip: Make online reservations early for cabins, screened shelters, and RV and tent sites. Places fill up year-round.

Camping at Garner State Park

Campground	No. of Sites	Max. Persons	Price per Night	Description
Pecan Grove	49 tent sites	8	$20.00	Old Garner. Picnic table, grill, fire ring, water.
Oakmont	39 RV sites	8	$26.00	Old Garner near river. Water and electricity.
Persimmon Hill	75 tent sites	8	$15.00	New Garner. Picnic table, grill, fire ring, water.
Rio Frio	99 RV sites	8	$22.00	New Garner. Water and 30-amp hookups. Picnic table, grill, fire ring.
Live Oak	73 RV sites	8	$26.00	New Garner. Water and 50-amp hookups.
Shady Meadows		8		Near Visitor Center. Overflow camping.
River Crossing		8		Near Visitor Center. Overflow camping.
Cypress Springs	1 group site	40	$350.00	New Garner. Group dining hall, 5 screened shelters (each sleeps 8 on bunk beds).

Note: Each site has nearby hot showers and restrooms.

Camping under the trees is popular at Garner State Park. Photo by Thomas C. Self.

Reservations for cabins and screen shelters go fast. Photo by Thomas C. Self.

Cabins and Screen Shelters at Garner State Park

Type	No. of Sites	Fee per Night	Description
Cabin without fireplace	4	$130.00	Kitchen, but no utensils or dishes. Bathroom with shower. AC/heat. No linens. Max.: 6 people. Cabin 18 is ADA-compliant.
Cabin with fireplace	13	$150.00	Kitchen, but no utensils or dishes. Bathroom with shower. AC/heat. No linens. Max.: 6 people.
Screen shelter (New Garner)	16	$30.00	Shower and restroom nearby.
Screen shelter (Old Garner)	21	$35.00	Shower and restroom nearby.

Lost Maples State Natural Area

RR 187, off US 83, near Leakey
830–966–3413
texas.reserveworld.com (reservations)
www.tpwd.texas.gov/state-parks/lost-maples
Hours: Daily
Fees: $6:00; additional fees for overnight stays

A large, isolated stand of bigtooth maples turns this area into a brilliant show of color from late October to mid-November every year. Viewing the gorgeous fall colors, or "leaf peeping," as they say in New England, is a very popular activity, especially on fall weekends. This 2,174-acre park, located 58 miles northeast of Uvalde, contains a wide variety of landscapes, including limestone canyons, plateau grasslands, maple forests, and clear streams. There are plenty of picnic tables for day use. If you don't find one at first, keep walking down the terraces toward the stream.

Lost Maples State Natural Area offers primitive camping as well as tent and RV sites with water and electricity. Photo by Thomas C. Self.

Geocaching

Geocaching is high-tech scavenger hunting using GPS devices. There are many caches in this area, and hunting them can be fun for the whole family. There are apps available for smart phones that will help you on your next hunt. Ask for information at the park entrance. To learn how geocaching works, visit www.tpwd.texas.gov/spdest/activities/outdoor_recreation/geocache.

Camping

With over fifty primitive, backcountry campsites, Lost Maples State Natural Area lures backpack campers with its quiet outback. Tent and RV campers can also be accommodated in a shady campground that is wheelchair accessible.

Hiking

Discover bigtooth maples, bald cypress, and sycamore trees along the spring-fed Sabinal River. As you transition upward on the rocky slopes, you'll be rewarded with scenic views and spectacular rock faces. There are a couple of steep areas, so be prepared with plenty of water and good hiking shoes.

Camping at Lost Maples State Natural Area

Type	No. of Sites	Fee per Night	Description
Primitive	40	$10.00	Hike-in only. No improvements.
Tent and RV	30	$20.00	Water, electricity, picnic table, nearby restrooms.

Hiking Trails at Lost Maples State Natural Area

Trail Name	Distance	Time	Rating	Description
Maple	0.36 mile	20 min.	Easy	See old bigtooth maples along this popular route.
East-West	1.0 mile	45 min.	Easy	Hike along a shaded tributary of the Sabinal River.
East	3.08 miles	3 hours	Challenging	Discover bigtooth maples, bald cypress, and sycamore trees along the spring-fed Sabinal River. As you move upward on the rocky slopes, you'll be rewarded with scenic views and spectacular rock faces. There are a couple of steep areas, so be prepared with plenty of water and good hiking shoes.
West	3.57 miles	3.5 hours	Challenging	Find fresh springs in the hills and spectacular views on this steep hike. Enjoy the beautiful Mystic Canyon area, but watch your step.
West Loop	2.37 miles (round trip)	1.5 hours	Moderate	Take a detour over to this shady and peaceful Ashe juniper grove.

Kickapoo Cavern State Park

FR 674, about 22 miles north of Brackettville
830–563–2342
texas.reserveworld.com (reservations)
www.tpwd.texas.gov/state-parks/kickapoo-cavern

Hours: Friday through Monday only; gates open between 8:00 a.m. and 5:00 p.m.

Entrance Fees: $3.00 day use, plus $10.00 for cave tour

Pro-tip: Do not enter caves without a guide.

In 1889 a Methodist circuit rider named Hal Cunningham and a group of friends "discovered" what is today Kickapoo Cavern. Relying on lantern light, they first entered "the Egyptian darkness of the subterranean wonder." Historic graffiti and layers of torch soot in the depths of the cave document explorations that began around 120 years ago during the time of European settlement. A large mound of burned rock and chipped stone near Kickapoo Cavern records visitation by prehistoric Native American groups. In dry periods a small pool deep within the cavern likely provided them with water. Although the cavern was presumably named for the Kickapoo Indians, archaeologists are unsure whether this historic tribe actually visited the cave. The park was ranchland until 1986, when the state acquired the property. The 6,368.4-acre park opened to the public in 2010.

Kickapoo Cavern Cave Tour

Hours: Saturdays, 1:00 p.m., year-round

Fee: $10.00

Reservations: required

Pro-tip: Wear sturdy hiking boots or walking shoes for the cave tour, and bring two flashlights per person. Each person will be issued a hard hat that must be worn. Dress lightly.

Guided flashlight tours of undeveloped Kickapoo Cavern are available on scheduled dates through advance reservation only. Participants can see the largest "speleothem" in Texas—a natural column formation rising as tall as an eight-story building. Although the cave is now mostly dry, dripping water once played an important role in shaping this and other formations, such as icicle-like stalactites and stalagmites, rippled sheets of flowstone, and moon-milk that resembles white cream cheese.

Kickapoo Cavern is a natural cave with no improvements like sidewalks, handrails, or lighting. This is a wild cave, not a show cave like Carlsbad Caverns. The temperature inside the cave is about 70 degrees year-round and can be humid due to water dripping through the porous limestone formations. The hike into the cave is moderately strenuous and not recommended for young children or those with mobility and health concerns. The tour requires fair hiking ability, and all participants must sign a liability release and wear sturdy hiking boots or walking shoes as well as carry two light sources per person. Unauthorized entry into the caves at the park is prohibited.

Guided tours of Kickapoo Cavern introduce hikers to a natural underground environment. Courtesy Texas Parks and Wildlife Department.

Stuart Bat Cave

Hours: sunset from April through October
Fee: $3.00 for entrance permit

Stuart Bat Cave is accessible to everyone, including those in wheelchairs. The cave is home to almost a million Mexican free-tailed bats that roost deep within the cave from spring through fall. At dusk the air comes alive with a flutter of bat wings as these flying mammals stream into the night in search of insects. The visitor center has binoculars to loan. Visitors can drive to the cave and park in the parking lot.

There is a diverse array of wildlife in the park. Some of the mammals more commonly seen include white-tailed deer, raccoons, ringtails, gray foxes, rock squirrels, porcupines, rabbits, various rodents, and of course, bats. The park has become popular for locating hard-to-find birds such as gray vireo, varied bunting, and Montezuma quail. Kickapoo Caverns State Park is home to one of the largest breeding populations of endangered black-capped vireos on state-owned lands. Various uncommon species of reptiles and amphibians also live in the park.

The endangered black-capped vireo nests at Kickapoo Cavern State Park. Photo by Greg Lasley.

Camping

Fee: $12.00–$20.00

All of the park's twenty campsites have water, picnic tables, and barbecue grills. Four sites have RV hookups. Tents are welcome. There are flush toilets and good showers, but no trash disposal. Please carry out all your own trash.

Campsites at Kickapoo Cavern State Park

Type	No. of Sites	Fee per Night	Description
Tent only	11	$12.00	Water, picnic table, fire ring or grill, cement slab.
RV or tent	4	$20.00	Water, electricity, and sewer hookups, picnic table, fire ring or grill, cement slab.
Group site	5	$12.00	Each site accommodates 6 people. Five picnic tables, four water faucets, three grills, two fire rings.

Hiking, Bird-Watching, Biking

Pro-tip: To protect the black-capped vireo and its habitat, visitors are restricted to roads and trails during the breeding season, which lasts from March 15 to September 15. Some trails are under construction. Most trails are primitive and unmarked. Pick up a field checklist of birds at the visitor center.

Hiking Trails at Kickapoo Cavern State Park

Name	Length	Description
Kickapoo Cavern Road	1 mile	Guided hike. Reservations required.
South Gate Road	2.1 miles	Nice, easy biking road.
Seargeant Memorial Trail	0.8 mile	Moderate hike gains about 200 feet in elevation. Great view of the valley from the shade shelter overlooking the campgrounds.
The Long Way Home	4.0 miles	Mostly flat with areas of woods intermixed with open areas. Nice variation of habitats.
Pine Canyon Loop	2 miles	Hike and bike trail through partly open areas to piñon pines. Great pine fragrance.
Barbado Ridge Trail	1.5 miles	Hike from the valley floor up about 1,900 feet to the top of the ridge. Good for spotting Montezuma quail and viewing great sunsets.
Indigo Creek Connection	1.7 miles	Fairly flat. Good for birding, especially black-capped vireos and gray vireos.
Vireo Vista	0.4 mile	Connects to Indigo Creek. Great for bird-watching.
Armadillo Lookout Trail	0.4 mile	Great view of the whole park. Off Vireo Vista Trail.
Stuart Bat Cave Cutoff	0.8 mile	Hike and bike through some shade to Stuart Cave.

Seminole Canyon State Park and Historic Site

US 90, west of Comstock

432–292–4464

512–389–9000 or texas.reserveworld.com (reservations)

www.twpd.texas.gov/state-parks/seminole-canyon

Hours: daily, year-round; office: 8:00 a.m.–4:45 p.m.; park gate closes at 10:00 p.m.

Fees: $3.00 day use; additional fee for camping

Pro-tip: No hiking is allowed in Seminole Canyon itself without a guide. Temperatures can easily reach 90 degrees F or more almost any time of year, especially in the canyon. Tent camping and lengthy hiking are not recommended during the summer.

This shaman sculpture by Bill Worrell welcomes visitors to Seminole Canyon. Photo by author.

Seminole Canyon State Park and Historic Site is a great place to learn more about rock art and the Chihuahuan Desert. Enjoy hiking, mountain biking, camping, rock art tours, historical study, nature viewing, and the great little museum overlooking the spectacular canyon. The museum has wonderful exhibits on the prehistoric people who one lived here, the Chinese workers who built the 1883 railroad, early ranching and sheep raising, and the natural environment. The park, with over 2,000 acres near the Rio Grande, opened to the public in 1980. Fate Bell Shelter in the canyon contains some of North America's oldest Native American pictographs and is one of the oldest cave dwellings in North America. See more in the chapter on rock art.

Hiking Trails at Seminole Canyon State Park and Historic Site

Trail	Length	Time	Difficulty	Description
Windmill Nature Trail	0.75 mile	30 min.	Moderate	Hiking trail to an old spring.
ADA Birding Trail	0.1 mile	15 min.	Easy	Paved trail to birding station.
Canyon Rim Trail	7.5 miles	3.5 hours	Strenuous	Hike along the rim of Seminole Canyon and the Rio Grande.
Presa Overlook Trail	3 miles	1.5 hours	Moderate	Hike an old ranch road to the Presa Canyon Overlook.
Rio Grande Trail	6 miles	3 hours	Moderate	Hike an old ranch road to the confluence of Seminole Canyon and the Rio Grande.
Middle Fork Trail	1 mile	30 min.	Moderate	Connects Rio Grande Trail and Presa Overlook Trail.

Hiking in the canyon itself is limited to guided tours and requires an additional fee. There are plenty of upland trails you can hike by yourself, however, especially when the weather is cool. Hiking boots, hiking stick, hat, sunscreen, and water are recommended year-round. Pick up a birding list at the visitor center.

Camping

Fee: $8.00–$20.00 per night

Pro-tip: Bring extra tarps and rope to create a shaded picnic table space. Stake your tent down well and put on the rainfly. With any luck at all your tent will stay put instead of blowing over. Tent camping is extremely hot in summer.

In cool weather you can't miss with any one of the forty-six campsites available. All have a beautiful view of the desert, and the night sky is amazing! There are no trees or natural shade, however, so be prepared. The shower house is clean and easily accessible from all sites. All sites have picnic tables, fire rings, and tent pads. Even if your site doesn't have water immediately nearby, there are plenty of faucets all around the camping area. Reservations are required. Be forewarned: the wind can blow really hard out here.

4

Rock Art

The ancient people of Southwest Texas left many traces of their lives for us to contemplate. Some of the oldest art in the world has been found here, though much of it cannot be seen today. The most extensive, complex, and accessible examples are found in the dry Lower Pecos Canyonlands. Painted images cover the walls of rock-shelters, or shallow overhangs in canyon walls, in the Lower Pecos at over 300 documented spots. These images may be the oldest paintings in North America, dating to at least 4,000 years ago. International experts agree these paintings are irreplaceable artifacts of human cultural heritage.

"Rock art" includes painted images, known as pictographs, and petroglyphs, which are carved, pecked, or incised images in stone. Both types occur in Southwest Texas, as well as mobile art, or art that could be carried around in the form of painted pebbles.

Ancient polychrome images are painted in many rock-shelters of the Lower Pecos Canyonlands. Photo by Stephen L. Black.

Please note that it is against federal antiquities law to remove any ancient art from its setting. So please be respectful when viewing any of these treasures.

The vast majority of rock art sites are on private property and thus are not available to the public. Trespassing is a serious offense and has been known to be met with a rifle. All rock art sites are extremely fragile, and even the touch of a finger leaves oils from the skin that can deteriorate the painting. Even human breath can damage the delicate images. The rock art of the Lower Pecos Canyonlands is one of the most outstanding cultural remains in the world, and seeing it in person is an unforgettable experience. We must be good stewards of the past if we want this art to be seen by future generations.

Pictographs

There are four major styles of pictographs in the Lower Pecos Canyonlands: Pecos River, Red Linear, Red Monochrome, and Historic. The only way to see four of these styles is to join the Rock Art Foundation (www.rockart.org) and go on some of their exclusive tours. For a good look at the Pecos River style, take the tour at Seminole Canyon State Park and Historic Site, which is open to everyone (with some restrictions for young children and health or mobility issues), or show up at the gate to the White Shaman Preserve on Saturday at noon for the Rock Art Foundation's weekly guided tour.

Pecos River Style

The oldest and most complex style is known as Pecos River style. This style of painting is at least 4,000 years old and is distinguished by the use of multiple colors, or polychrome. Red, orange, yellow, white, and black can still be discerned today.

The Pecos River style of rock art uses red, yellow, white, and black. Courtesy Shumla Archaeological Research and Education Center.

The colored pigments were made from naturally occurring minerals. Red, orange, and yellow came from ochers; white from kaolin, and black from manganese. The nearest source of kaolin is in the Big Bend area, so traders must have traveled back and forth many thousands of years ago in order to obtain white for the paint. Once the pigments were ground, they were mixed with fat, probably from the marrow of deer bones, to make a thick paste. The paint was thinned lightly with a soapy substance that comes from yucca roots to make it easier to spread.

Current researchers believe the colors themselves had spiritual significance to the original painters. These paintings were usually done as murals or panels on the back walls and overhanging roofs of rock-shelters, and some can be 100 feet long or more. Some of the large figures are depictions of humans and animals, and some are abstract and enigmatic, so they are not easy to interpret. They are fascinating and raise questions about who made them and what they mean. No one knows exactly who the painters were or what they called themselves. Yet these ancient people call to us through their paintings even today. If not for their art, they would most likely be all but forgotten.

Red Linear Style

Red Linear style is identified by small, red stick figures, often in hidden places like secluded walls. The figures are often whimsical and seem to be dancing or engaged in other group activities. The figures are only a few inches tall. The name of the people who painted in this style is not known.

Small, red stick figures identify the Red Linear style. Courtesy Shumla Archaeological Research and Education Center.

Red Monochrome Style

Red Monochrome style made its entrance into the Lower Pecos between AD 1000 and 1600. Many researchers believe this style was introduced by newcomers to the area, but again researchers do not know the name of these people. Red, fairly realistic figures of humans and animals are hallmarks of this style. Some human male figures hold bows and arrows, and naturalistic animals such as deer, dogs, rabbits, mountain lions, turtles, bison, catfish, and turkeys are easily identified.

Naturalistic people and animals characterize the Red Monochrome style. Courtesy Shumla Archaeological Research and Education Center.

Historic Style

When the Apache, Comanche, Kickapoo, and Kiowa encountered the Spanish in the Lower Pecos Canyonlands sometime after AD 1600, they began to represent the European strangers in paint. The Historic style includes paintings of horses, guns, churches, and Spaniards wearing hats, shoes, and belt buckles. Often these were painted on top of other preexisting rock art styles.

After AD 1600 Native Americans depicted Spanish explorers in their work. Courtesy Shumla Archaeological Research and Education Center.

Petroglyphs

A large petroglyph site exists on private property at Lewis Canyon on the Pecos River. Hundreds of abstract, geometric glyphs were pecked or scratched into the flat bedrock sometime between AD 1 and 1000. Documentation is currently ongoing, but at least two distinct styles have been discovered. The Discrete Geometric style is angular, abstract, geometric, and enigmatic. Straight lines, arcs, and circles predominate. The Serpentine style is more sinuous and graceful. Curved lines, circles, and spirals accompany human stick figures, animal tracks, and human footprints.

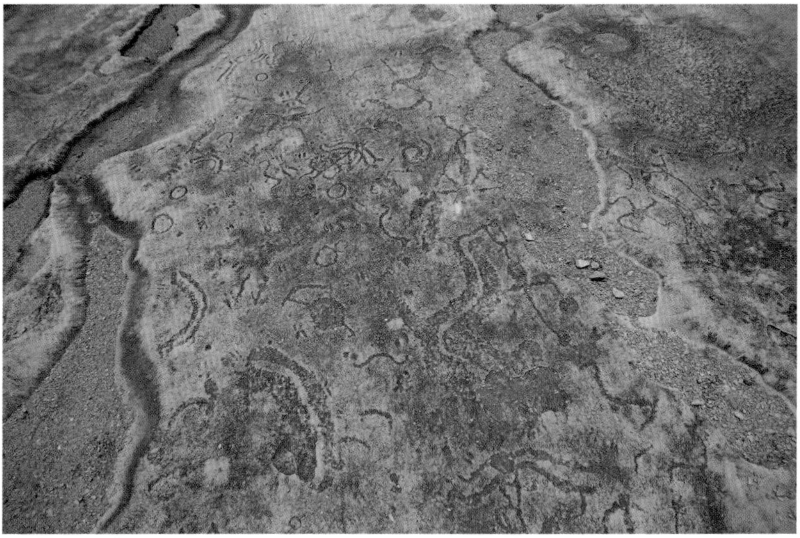

Geometric glyphs were pecked on this stone floor sometime between AD 1 and 1000. Courtesy Shumla Archaeological Research and Education Center.

Who Made the Rock Art?

Even though some researchers believe the people who made Lower Pecos rock art were Western Uto-Aztecan speakers, we will never know the name they called themselves. Their actual language has long passed from human memory. Archaeologists have learned a lot about their daily lives, however, through painstaking analysis of the cast-off bits and flotsam found buried in the many archaeological sites in the area. The people were hunter-gatherers, which simply means they found all their food and resources in the natural environment around them. They had no agriculture, metal, or pottery.

Their most long-lasting tools were made of stone. Flint, or chert, found in abundance in the Edwards Plateau and many other areas, provided fine material for knapping sharp knives and spear points. Many other tools were made of plant materials, such as rope and twine twisted from lechugilla fiber. Baskets as well as mats for sitting or sleeping were woven from sotol fiber. Animal hides provided leather and fur for garments.

Many of the rock-shelters were occupied at various times, but the people also made temporary camps on the uplands, perhaps for hunting. Undoubtedly they camped by the rivers as well, but most evidence of that has been washed away by ancient floods.

Ancient people who lived in a rock shelter known as the Kincaid Site along the Sabinal River left mysterious painted and incised pebbles behind. Some of the pebbles have clear circular or straight-line designs scratched in them, and some are more difficult to discern. A few of the small rocks have remnants of red pigment, indicating they were painted or scratched into red ochre stones themselves. Likely the painted stones were used ceremonially in some way, but exactly how, we'll never know. Researchers do not know the name these people called themselves, or what happened to them. But clearly they had complex thoughts that were expressed in portable art, such as these stones. It is possible that the people also painted on hides, walls, faces, and bodies, but traces of such work no longer exist.

At least 13,000 years ago the people at this same site hauled limestone cobbles up from the river below to pave the floor of the shelter and keep it dry. Most likely they added layers of plant material and hides on top of that to make a comfortable living surface. The bone of an extinct Pleistocene horse was found lying directly on top of this flooring, enabling archaeologists to determine a clear date. This cobblestone floor is considered one of the oldest construction sites in North America.

Native peoples along the Sabinal River had many choices for hunting and gathering. They hunted mammoth, ancient bison, camels, horses, and other large game at the end of the last Ice Age as well as alligators and aquatic turtles. Nuts, seeds, roots, and leaves were also abundant. The shelter itself was badly looted by modern humans, and much of its story is lost. Please be mindful of the past as you travel this area and respect both cultural heritage and private property. The best way to learn more about this site is by visiting the website Texas Beyond History at www.texasbeyondhistory.net, which has an extensive online gallery as well as activities for kids. No other public exhibit is available.

Where to See Rock Art

Seminole Canyon State Park and Historic Site

US 90, just past Comstock
432–292–4464
www.tpwd.state.tx.us/state-parks/seminole-canyon
Hours: daily, year-round
Fees: $3.00 for day use, plus $5.00 for tours
What you can see: Fate Bell Shelter, Panther Cave, Presa Canyon
Pro-tip: No hiking is allowed in the canyon itself without a guide. Wear a hat; take water and, of course, a camera. Boots are recommended, but sneakers will work. Never disturb artifacts or touch ancient rock art. Even the oils in your fingers will damage the paintings.

The most accessible place to see Pecos River style rock art is Seminole Canyon State Park and Historic Site. Some of North America's oldest Native

Seminole Canyon holds magnificent rock art in its shelters. Photo by author.

American pictographs and one of the oldest cave dwellings are located in Seminole Canyon.

The guided tour to Fate Bell Shelter goes every Wednesday through Sunday. September 1 through May 31 tours leave at 10:00 a.m. and 3:00 p.m. Due to high temperatures in summer, the tour is available only at 10:00 a.m. from June through August.

The moderate hike takes you into the canyon, into the rock-shelter, and up close to magnificent polychrome paintings thousands of years old. This hike is not recommended for small children or people with medical conditions because some places are steep, and it can be very hot.

Fate Bell Shelter was occupied for thousands of years by hunters and gatherers who painted the entire back wall, floor to ceiling, with images in red, orange, yellow, black, and white. Much of this painting is gone today due to the ravages of time and the environment. In some cases, the painting has also been destroyed by modern vandals.

The largest and brightest remaining figures are near one end of the shelter wall. The grouping consists of at least four figures. A central figure appears to have black "wings" on either side that are held out by "attendants." The

Visitors see a glimpse of an ancient world at Seminole Canyon. Photo by author.

central figure has a large head with deer antlers on each side above the ears. The figure has legs and brushlike strokes for toes. Bear paws, feathers, or other ornamentation sits on the shoulders. The so-called attendant toward the main length of the wall is outlined in red with a black center line. Two legs and feet may also be seen. The attendant nearer the end of the wall is less clear, but appears to be outlined in red with a black stripe down one side and white on the other. Behind the black "wing" nearer the end of the wall is the fourth figure, which is larger than the other three. Below the wing, look for the legs and feet. The body rises above the wing, and the arms appear outstretched. A bundle or ornament hangs from the arm nearer the end of the wall. An atlatl, or spear-thrower, with a large weight and an attached spear is just beyond the arm.

While you are in the park, you can also take the rather strenuous 7.5-mile Canyon Rim trail. Use the telescope at the end of the trail to view the magnificent figures in Panther Cave. Allow at least 3.5 hours, take water, and be prepared for weather. There is very little shade along this trail, and the hike is not recommended for small children or people with medical conditions, but the rock art is spectacular. If you are boating on Lake Amistad, you may be able to view the site from the water as well.

Many painted rock-shelters are in rugged locations. Photo by Jean Clottes; courtesy Shumla Archaeological Research and Education Center.

The Panther Cave painting is huge, stretching over 130 feet on the back wall of the shelter. Once over forty figures could be seen, but serious damage from water, mineral stains, insects, and spalling, or flaking off, has occurred. Eight feline figures have been identified in the cave, and some are quite large. A large red cat gives the shelter its common name.

See the park's website or call the park directly to find out about occasional tours to other pictograph sites in Presa Canyon, just off Seminole Canyon, and others. Each of these tours requires a reservation and an additional fee. For more on other hiking and camping opportunities in the state park, see the chapter on state parks.

Galloway White Shaman Preserve

US 90, just east of the Pecos River High Bridge
www.rockart.org
Hours: Saturdays, 12:00 p.m., year-round
Fees: suggested donation: $20 per person
What you can see: White Shaman panel
Pro-tip: Besides the usual hat, water, camera, boots, and sunscreen, also bring sandwiches to eat before or after your hike. There is no place to eat for at least 25 miles, and you're going to be hungry. Also a hiking stick would be good if you have one. Portable toilet facilities are located only at the trailhead.

The White Shaman painting overlooks the Pecos River. Photo by Thomas C. Self.

Meet at the gate on US 90 just east of the Pecos River bridge around noon. The tour leaves the parking area around 12:30 p.m. every Saturday. Don't be late, or you'll be disappointed. Tours are offered by well-versed volunteers from the Rock Art Foundation, which owns the property. Tours are limited to about twenty people. If you have a larger group, please call ahead to make arrangements. The hike is fairly strenuous, and boots are recommended. At one point, you will have to pull yourself up a slick rock by a rope, so moderately good fitness is a plus. Don't worry;

this author has been pushed and dragged up before, so if that happens to you, you've got company. The tour takes two to three hours, depending on the crowd. Not recommended for small children or people with medical conditions.

Making the hike up to the small shelter overlooking the Pecos River is part of the experience of viewing the painting. It was always difficult to reach and was probably located there on purpose. The mural fills a wall approximately 13 by 26 feet. Many figures are easily visible, including a large "catfish"-like motif in the middle along with a white human-like figure that gave the shelter its name. Instead of representing a shaman, however, the white figure may denote Venus or the moon goddess, according to a recent theory. The White Shaman panel, as it is called, is one of the most spectacular paintings in the world and will introduce you to a whole new way of thinking.

The Witte Museum, located in San Antonio, offers additional tours to many fascinating sites in the area. These tours require registration and additional fees. Hiking with the Witte Museum is the only way to see the Lewis Canyon petroglyphs and various historic sites. See their website at www.wittemuseum.org to register for tours and for more information.

Devils River State Natural Area

Off Texas 277, about 65 miles from Del Rio
1–800–395–2256 (tour reservations)
www.tpwd.texas.gov/state-parks/devils-river

Park staff lead tours to various rock art sites, including Ascension Shelter, within the state natural area. Tours generally run about three hours long, traveling by high-clearance vehicle, with some walking. Advance reservations are required, as tours depend on staff availability. When this book went to press, there was no fee for the tours.

5

Historic Forts

Starting in 1849, the US Army built a series of forts in Southwest Texas to protect the border with Mexico and the western frontier. Today travelers can visit Fort Clark in Brackettville, Fort Duncan in Eagle Pass, and Fort Inge in Uvalde to see remains of cavalry stables, barracks, mess halls, and administration buildings of the past. Anyone interested in military history, Medal of Honor winners, African American history, or Black Seminole Indian scouts will find much to think about here. Pick up a Texas Forts Trail map at the Judge Roy Bean Visitor Center in Langtry.

Fort Clark

Fort Clark Springs, US 90
Brackettville, TX 78832
830–563–9340
www.fortclark.com

History

Fort Clark was an important part of the US system of defense in the Southwest from 1852 to 1946. The fort was home to many infantry and cavalry regiments, including the 9th and 10th Cavalry and Black Seminole Indian scouts. Originally established to protect stage routes, units from Fort Clark saw action in various Indian campaigns in the United States and Mexico. Early in the Civil War the volunteer Provisional Army of Texas briefly occupied the fort. Over 12,000 US Army troops were posted at Fort Clark before shipping out to Europe in 1944 during World War II. A section of Fort Clark was also briefly designated as a German prisoner of war camp. The end of horse cavalry led to deactivation of the post in 1946.

The US Army realized the strategic potential of Las Moras Springs, which brought many Native American groups to the area. Fort Clark was established at that spot to protect the border from Mexico and guard the Chihuahua Road, sometimes called the Comanche War Trail.

African Americans known by the Native Americans as "Buffalo Soldiers" served at Fort Clark after the Civil War in the 9th and 10th Cavalry. Black Seminole Indian scouts served at Fort Clark from 1870 to 1914. Under Lt. John L. Bullis, who commanded them from 1873 to 1881, the scouts played decisive roles in many Indian campaigns, including excursions into Mexico. Col. Ranald Mackenzie led attacks from Fort Clark against Kickapoo and Lipan Apaches at the village of Remolino in Mexico in 1873. Other well-known military men connected with Fort Clark include "Pecos Bill" Shafter, who led Indian raids into Mexico during 1876–78; Gen. William T. Sherman, who visited on an inspection tour in 1882; Gen. George S. Patton, who served as regimental commander in 1938; and Brig. Gen. Jonathan Wainwright, under whose authority the present swimming pool was built in 1939.

The Fort Clark Commissary served the cavalrymen there until 1946. Photo by Thomas C. Self.

Most of the remaining limestone buildings of the fort date to the 1870s, but the old post headquarters building dates back to 1857. For more complete information on Fort Clark, see www.texasbeyondhistory.net. The fort is now part of the Fort Clark Springs resort and retirement community. For more information about recreational opportunities at Fort Clark Springs that are open to the public, see the entry for Brackettville in the Towns chapter.

BUFFALO SOLDIERS

Soldiers of African American descent in the US Army were known as "Buffalo Soldiers" after the Civil War and until the end of World War I. They were often confronted with racial prejudice from both the military and civilians. Attacks on Buffalo Soldiers occurred in several places along the Texas-Mexico border as well as in Houston from 1899 to 1917. More than twenty Buffalo Soldiers throughout the United States have received the Medal of Honor, the highest number of any US military unit.

Buffalo Soldiers led by Gen. John Pershing participated in the Mexican Expedition into Mexico to capture Pancho Villa during the Mexican Revolution in 1916. They were involved in the Battle of Carrizal in Chihuahua, Mexico. Several were taken captive and later released. General Pershing was known as "Black Jack" Pershing because of his leadership and the admiration of African American troops.

Black Seminole Indian scouts served in the 24th Infantry Regiment at Fort Clark. Courtesy Fort Clark Historical Society of Kinney County.

BLACK SEMINOLES

The 24th Infantry Regiment at Fort Clark was a special group known as Black Seminoles for their mixed heritage as descendants of free blacks and escaped slaves from the United States and Seminole Indians in Florida and Oklahoma. Black Seminole leader John Horse led about 180 people to northern Mexico in 1849 to escape slave hunters in the United States. Black Seminoles primarily served as Indian scouts during the American Indian Wars after being recruited by the US Army in 1870. Scouts in the 24th Infantry Regiment were famous for their tracking abilities and feats of endurance. After discharge from the army, many Black Seminoles remained in the Brackettville area. The town remains a center of Black Seminole history and culture.

Four Black Seminole Indian scouts won the Medal of Honor and are buried in the Seminole Indian Scout Cemetery, located in Brackettville. John Ward, Pompey Factor, and Isaac Payne (or Paine) were recruited into the US Army around 1870 from their home in Mexico. In April 1975 their commander, Lt. John L. Bullis, led them to scout for Indian raiders in the area. After four days they found a fresh track, and on April 25, a half mile from the mouth of the Pecos River, they engaged a party of about twenty-five Comanche Indians with dozens of horses. Outgunned and outnumbered, the scouts withdrew, but Bullis's horse bolted, stranding him. Factor and Payne, who served as the trumpeter, provided cover fire, and Ward rescued his lieutenant. All three were awarded the Medal of Honor for their actions.

Isaac Payne remained in the army until 1901, when he moved back to Mexico. Ward was discharged from the army in 1894 and lived as a farmer the rest of his life. Factor served in the Red River War in the Texas Panhandle with Col. Ranald McKenzie to remove the Comanche, Kiowa, Southwestern Cheyenne, and Arapaho Indians to Indian Territory in Oklahoma. In 1877 Factor was involved in an incident with fellow scout Adam Payne (no known relation to Isaac) in which shots were fired. Factor fled to Mexico but later surrendered and rejoined the US Army. He remained in the army until 1880. Isaac Payne remained in the army until 1901, when he moved back to Mexico.

The fourth Black Seminole scout to win the Medal of Honor was Adam Payne (or Paine). He joined the US Army at Fort Duncan near Eagle Pass in 1873. He participated in the Red River War against the Indians in the Panhandle in 1874. He received the Medal of Honor for "rending invaluable service" to Col. McKenzie on October 13, 1877. Payne was killed on January

1, 1877, by Claron A. Windus, a fellow Medal of Honor recipient, who was serving as deputy sheriff of Brackettville. Windus was attempting to arrest Payne as a murder suspect when he shot him.

Claron Augustus Windus (1850–1927)

Windus served as a drummer boy during the Civil War, a bugler during the Indian Wars, and a captain in the Spanish-American War. He received the Medal of Honor for his actions on July 12, 1870, during a battle with Kiowa Indians in northern Texas.

He was discharged from the army in 1871 and became deputy sheriff in Brackettville. In 1877 he shot fellow Medal of Honor recipient Adam Payne (or Paine) as Windus attempted to arrest Payne for murder.

In 1898 Windus volunteered as a commissioned officer and served with the 9th US Infantry Regiment during the Spanish-American War. He is buried in the Masonic Cemetery in Brackettville.

FORT CLARK DAYS

Usually in March every year
www.fortclarkdays.org

Buffalo Soldier reenactors and others present two days of living history with live music and fun every year. Check the website in February for exact dates.

FORT CLARK MUSEUM

830–563–2493
Hours: Saturdays and Sundays, 1:00 p.m.–4:00 p.m.
Admission: free; donations appreciated
The old guardhouse at Fort Clark features relics of cavalry and infantry soldiers as well as those of the Black Seminole Indian scouts. Exhibits present over a hundred years of fascinating military history from the Indian wars of the 1870s to World War II.

Visitors can almost see the uniformed commanders sitting by the fire at Fort Clark. Photo by author.

Fort Duncan

400 Garrison St.
Eagle Pass, TX 78852
830–773–3224

History

Just off South Monroe Street and Bliss Avenue in Eagle Pass, a few restored limestone buildings are all that remain of Fort Duncan, one of a string of US Army posts established along the border after the Mexican War of 1846. The site was listed in the National Register of Historic Places in 1971. Since it began in 1849, the fort has been opened and closed numerous times by the military.

Controlled by the Confederate Army during the Civil War, the fort was an important customs point for Confederate cotton and munitions trade with Mexico. By 1870 Black Seminole Indian scouts were attached to the command by the US Army. Over 16,000 troops were stationed here during World War I.

The city formally acquired the property in 1935 and converted it into Fort Duncan Park. In 1942 the mayor offered the fort to the military for use during World War II. The government accepted and used Fort Duncan for commissioned personnel stationed at Eagle Pass Army Air Field.

First US Military Cross-Country Flight

On March 3, 1911, Benjamin Foulois and Philip Orin Parmelee flew from Laredo to Fort Duncan in Eagle Pass on one leg of the US military's first cross-country reconnaissance flight. The Wright Model B covered 106 miles in two hours at an altitude of 800 feet.

FORT DUNCAN MUSEUM

310 Bliss Dr.
Eagle Pass, TX 78852
830–773–3224
Hours: Tuesday–Saturday, 11:00 a.m.–5:00 p.m.
Admission: donation requested

Artifacts and photographs of the life of soldiers on the frontier are on display at the museum, which is housed in the old post headquarters building.

Fort Inge

Fort Inge Historical Park
CR 375, off RR 140 (Pearsall Rd.), 1.5 miles south of Uvalde
http://www.fortwiki.com/Fort_Inge
Hours: Saturdays and Sundays, 8:00 a.m.–8:00 p.m.; self-guided walking tour available anytime
Admission: adults $2.00, children $1.00, or $5.00 per vehicle

To find the remains of Fort Inge, take US 83 south from Uvalde, which soon becomes Ranch Road 117. Turn slightly east onto Ranch Road 140 and go about 2 miles. Watch for a small sign for County Road 375. The road deteriorates as you go. You may wonder where you are by the time you come upon what's left of the small fort, just below a formidable lookout mountain. Watch for sleeping dogs in the road and old pickups during the last bit. The bleached-out walls of a log cabin are a mute reminder of the men who served in this lonesome spot. Artifacts from Fort Inge are displayed at the Janey Slaughter Briscoe Grand Opera House in Uvalde.

Lookouts had an unobstructed view for many miles from the hilltop at Fort Inge. Photo by Thomas C. Self.

History

Fort Inge was established in 1849 as part of the effort by the United States to secure the Mexican border after the Mexican War of 1846. The fort was named in honor of Lt. Zebulon M. P. Inge of the US Second Dragoons, killed at the Mexican War battle of Resaca de la Palma. The missions of the soldiers included security patrols for the construction of the San Antonio–El Paso military road, escorts for supply trains and mail, protection for frontier settlements from bandits and Indian raiders, and guarding the international boundary with Mexico. The fort was a typical one-company, fifty-man post for most of its history.

Fort Inge was on the Cotton Road to Eagle Pass, over which hundreds of wagons and oxcarts took cotton to Mexico in exchange for vital goods during the Union blockade of the South during the Civil War. The fort was part of the defense line from Brownsville to El Paso and was occupied by volunteer Confederate cavalry until federal troops reoccupied it in 1866. From 1868 to 1869, the fort was home to several units of African American Buffalo Soldiers.

After the fort was decommissioned in 1869, Texas Rangers used the site until 1884. In 1961 the site became Fort Inge Historical Site County Park. Archaeological evidence from investigations carried out in the early 1980s indicates that the site has been intermittently occupied since about 6000 BC. Ranching during the Spanish colonial and Mexican periods probably occurred as well.

Camp Dix, C.S.A.

Camp Dix, located 7 miles east of Uvalde and only 4.5 miles from Fort Inge, at a place called Black Waterhole, operated from 1862 to 1864 during the Civil War. The camp was part of a line of fortifications, each no more than a day's horseback ride from the next, that stretched from the Red River to the Rio Grande to protect frontier settlements and roads. Volunteers protected the nearby road to Mexico. Although Uvalde County voted 76 to 16 against secession, a number of men joined the Confederate Army. Some Unionists moved to Mexico. The war brought hard times and a rash of Indian attacks. In 1863–64, when the Union held the lower Rio Grande, Eagle Pass became the chief export city for the Confederacy, and wagon trains increased along the road. Often without food, clothing, horses, and ammunition, the Confederate and state troops, backed by citizens' posses, brought a measure of protection to this frontier region. Nothing is left of this short-lived outpost today. A historical marker is located at the intersection of Main Street and Getty in Uvalde.

6

Hunting

A hunter's paradise, Southwest Texas has some of the best hunting environments in North America. Texas has more white-tailed deer than any other state, and over fifty species of exotics. Feral hogs are abundant, as are turkeys and doves. You will need to start early to plan your hunting trip, however, as a hunting license is required of any person, regardless of age, who hunts any animal, bird, frog, or turtle in this state. Buy one at state parks, outfitters, or online at http://tpwd.texas.gov/business/licenses/online_sales.

Hunting seasons vary according to type of animal and region of the state. See the Texas Parks and Wildlife website at tpwd.texas.gov/huntwild/hunt/, or call 800–792–1112 or 512–389–4800, Monday through Friday between 8:00 a.m. and 5:00 p.m., with questions. You can also download the free Texas hunting app from the website.

Reservations on hunting ranches tend to fill up as soon as licenses are available for that year, so plan accordingly.

Southwest Texas is famous for the diversity of animal life living there. Hunting white-tailed deer, Rio Grande turkey, and many other species is popular in the Del Rio area in season. There are many private ranches and other organizations that allow hunting, but expect to pay premium prices. Accommodations vary. Contact ranches and outfitters directly for more information.

Southwest Texas is famous for deer-hunting. Photo by Thomas C. Self.

BowRanch

Grape Hollow on Nine Mile Road
Uvalde, TX 78801
830–279–8921
www.bowranch.com/

Located fifty minutes northeast of Uvalde, BowRanch offers free-range archery hunts for white-tailed deer, hogs, Rio Grande turkey, and aoudad sheep. The ranch has 2,000 acres of scenic Hill Country terrain complimented by springs and canyons. Accommodations include a nice cabin, electricity, hot water, Wi-Fi, walk-in cooler, hunting stands, and feeders. The BowRanch also offers lodging for nature tourism and photography. Summer rentals are also available.

Brushy Hill Trophy Bow Hunting Ranch

RR 187, 4 miles south of Sabinal
Sabinal, TX 78881
830–988–2802
www.brushyhill.com

Owner-operated 13,000-acre ranch with bow hunting only since 1994. Offers white-tailed deer, Rio Grande turkey, and year-round feral hog. Affordable pricing and no trophy fees. All hunts include lodging. Unlimited hog and predator hunting. Predominantly low fence.

Bug Scuffle Ranch

928 FM 337
Vanderpool, TX 78885
830–966–1581
www.bugscuffle.com

Bow hunting for white-tailed deer, axis deer, Catalina goats, Corsican sheep, Black Hawaiian sheep, blackbuck antelope, red stag, and Texas Dall sheep. Also wild hogs, predators, and varmints. Lodging available. No pets allowed.

Carter Country Ranch

TX 337
Leakey, TX 78873
830–597–3294
www.cartercountryranch.com

Guided and unguided hunts for exotic and domestic game animals for both experienced and inexperienced hunters. Children welcome, motorcycle friendly, tours, no pets, guest cabin year-round.

Double L Dove Hunt

1639 Country Road 303
Knippa, TX 78870
830–261–1921
www.doubleldovehunt.com

Over 400 acres, including sesame fields, milo fields, and native sunflower fields especially for dove hunting. Specializes in small group hunts, mainly for mourning doves. Day hunts only with no accommodations.

Elderado

420 W. Oppenheimer
Uvalde, TX 78801
830–317–0456
www.elderado.net

Package hunts available for all hunting seasons; up to forty hunters can be accommodated. Deer, dove, quail, turkey, hog, and upland hunts with onsite lodging, including eight bedrooms and seven baths. Facilities can be rented for parties in the off-season.

501 Ranch

Box 510
Uvalde, TX 78802
830–278–3939
www.501ranch.com

White-tailed deer, black buck antelope, turkey, quail, dove, and skeet shooting. Hunt on over 9,000 acres and enjoy the rustic lodge. The Nueces River runs through the property. The state's largest persimmon tree is also located here.

Hudspeth River Ranch

RR 163
Comstock, TX 78837
432–292–4637
www.hudspethriverranch.com

Located about 20 miles north of Comstock on the Devils River, Hudspeth River Ranch offers hunting for white-tailed deer, Rio Grande turkey, wild hog, aoudad sheep, and other exotics. Prices include lodging. Reservations are typically made more than a year in advance.

Southwest Texas has a variety of habitats for wildlife. Photo by Thomas C. Self.

Indianhead Ranch

3110 Indianhead Ranch Rd.
Del Rio, TX 78840
830–775–6481
www.indianheadranch.com

This 10,000-acre ranch on the Devils River and Lake Amistad offers lodging and guide service as well as hunting for white-tailed deer, turkey, and over fifteen species of exotics. The entrance is about 2.5 miles from Rough Canyon Marina.

OX Hunting Ranch

1946 Private Road 2485
Uvalde, TX 78801
830–275–4962
www.oxhuntingranch.com

This 18,000-acre hunting and adventure ranch offers something for the whole family. More than forty species range freely over the ranch, including some of the largest herds of axis deer, aoudad sheep, blackbuck antelope, and scimitar-horned oryx in the world. Bow hunting, rifle hunting, and night hunting are available with appropriate licenses. Adventure seekers can drive a World War II Sherman tank, shoot machine guns, or rappel down a mountain. Skeet shooting, kayaking, and swimming are also available. Kids can feed giraffes by hand, milk cows, or hunt for arrowheads while the adults take a yoga class or partake of other pursuits. Photographers are welcome as well. Beautiful lodging and gourmet dining are available. Facilities can be rented for weddings and parties.

Rock Canyon Ranch

Dolan Creek Road, off US 277
Del Rio, TX 78840
830–563–5473
www.huntrcr.com

This 13,500-acre ranch is located near Dolan Falls on the Devils River. The luxurious 7,000-square-foot hunting lodge was built in 2010 and accommodates up to twenty-six people. Each room has a private bath. A large patio features an outdoor hot tub. Hunting for white-tailed deer, turkey, axis deer, aoudad sheep, and other exotics is offered. The lodge can be reserved for weddings, meetings, or parties during off-season.

TC Outfitters

3045 US 90 East
Castroville, TX 78009
210–264–5818
www.tcsouthtexashunts.com

TC Outfitters offers hunting on over 20,000 acres, located in different counties, for trophy white-tailed deer, turkey, wild boar, dove, and wild bobwhite quail. Hunting includes lodging, meals, beverages, and guides. Call for more information.

3P Ranch

1026 CR 365
Uvalde, TX 78801
830–900–6559
www.3p-ranch.com

Hunting for deer, turkey, quail, and dove. Also fishing and bow hunting. Luxury accommodations. Call for more information.

War Horse Ranch

2604 Garner Field Road
Uvalde, TX 78801
830–275–0853 and 830–486–9012
www.warhorseranch.com

Package hunts for trophy white-tailed deer and forty species of exotics. Turkey and dove hunting on ranch as well as hunting concessions on over twenty other ranches totaling 30,000 acres. The main lodge is a Santa Fe–style building with adobe walls located on the Frio River. Fishing, recreational lodging, bird watching, and swimming also available.

7

Towns

The emergence and growth of cities and towns in Southwest Texas primarily depended on two things: water and the coming of the railroad. The same two things also caused some towns to turn to dust. Listings for restaurants and lodging are found in this chapter. The websites listed in chapter 1 are a good place to try for lodging in the Western Hill Country. Most resort cabins rent for several nights at a time and are reserved early. Tent and RV campsites are also very popular.

Fascination is around every corner in Southwest Texas. Photo by Thomas C. Self.

Barksdale

TX 55, between Rocksprings and Uvalde

Population: a few hundred (estimated)

History

Barksdale is an unincorporated village that does not have accurate census data. The community is named for Lewis Barksdale, who patented a league and a labor of land in the area in 1847. Before there was Barksdale, however, there was Dixie. The settlement was named for Camp Dixie, a Texas Ranger post near the road to Fort Inge. Jerusha Sanchez, a midwife for Nueces Canyon area who was widowed by Indians in the 1870s, was the first civilian settler. Next came Elizabeth Hill, whose eldest son was a military scout. Lewis Barksdale, a veteran of Republic of Texas wars, established his ranch here around 1876. When a post office was created in 1882 and named for Barksdale, the name Dixie disappeared from use. The town grew dramatically in the late 1980s as a number of housing subdivisions were built there. In 1990 Barksdale had 617 inhabitants and six businesses. By 2000 the population had grown to 1,081 with sixteen businesses, according to the Texas State Historical Association.

Settlers struggled to establish towns in much of Southwest Texas. Photo by Thomas C. Self.

Restaurants

CHICKEN COOP GRILL
TX 55
Barksdale, TX 78828
830–234–3244
Hours: 10:30 a.m.–9:00 p.m.; closed Thursdays and Sundays

Fried catfish, chicken-fried chicken, hamburgers. Cash only.

DANA'S HOT DOG HOUSE
25607 TX 55
Barksdale, TX 78828
830–234–5500
Hours: Friday and Saturday, 10:30 a.m.–8:00 p.m.; Sunday, 12:00 p.m.–6:00 p.m.

Burgers, dogs, nachos, and Frito pie. Many hot dog varieties, including New York and Chicago style, Junk Yard Dogs, Guacamole Dogs, and Sausage on a Stick. Cash only.

Lodging

NUECES RIVER MOTEL
TX 55 and Taylor St.
Barksdale, TX 78828
830–234–3648

Small, quiet motel next to the Nueces River.

Brackettville

US 90
Population: about 1,875

History

The settlement was founded as Las Moras in 1852 by Oscar Brackett to serve the US Army installation at Fort Clark (1852–1946). For more information about the fort, see the chapter on historic forts. The town was renamed Brackettville in 1873, when it received a US post office. The San

Antonio–El Paso Road stagecoach used to make a regular stop here about that time. The town was later by-passed by the railroad by ten miles and never grew much larger than it is now.

Places to Visit

FORT CLARK SPRINGS

US 90
Brackettville, TX 78832
830–563–9340
www.fortclark.com

Since 1971, Fort Clark and the surrounding area has been operated as a private recreation and retirement community by the Fort Clark Springs Association. Visitors are welcome, and guards will issue a pass to persons interested in seeing the springs, touring the grounds, or using some of the recreational facilities.

Fort Clark is home to the third-largest spring-fed swimming pool in Texas. Las Moras Springs feeds the beautiful, crystal-clear pool and keeps the water a constant 68 degrees year-round. Access to the pool is included with a motel stay as well as RV or tent camping, or you can purchase a day pass for $5.00.

The water of Las Moras Springs drew people to the Brackettville area. Photo by Thomas C. Self.

Also on the grounds are two golf courses: an eighteen-hole course ($22.00 per day) and a nine-hole par 3 course ($10.00). Bring your own clubs, but golf carts are available for rent at the pro shop.

Over 21 miles of trails crisscross the 1,600-acre property at Fort Clark, including a 7-mile trail winding along the shaded Las Moras Creek. Bikes and horses are allowed on the trails, but no motorized vehicles. A bird list is available at the office. Watch for both axis and white-tailed deer.

Wild turkeys roam Fort Clark unafraid of visitors. Photo by Thomas C. Self.

Alamo Village

Alamo Village was a full-scale movie set constructed for John Wayne's movie *The Alamo* in the late 1950s, just 6 miles from Brackettville on Ranch Road 674. Over 100 movies were filmed there. The authentic replica of the Alamo compound, as it was in 1836 (the real thing is in San Antonio, of course), and surrounding village, included a cantina, a blacksmith shop, a jail, and an Indian store in addition to the mission itself. More than a million adobe bricks were required for construction as well as 14 miles of gravel roads. In between movies, the set was open as a tourist attraction with live music and stage shows. Reenactors engaged with tourists, and a herd of longhorn cattle was driven down the main street from time to time. Sadly, Alamo Village is now permanently closed.

MONTALVO HOUSE

103 E. Thomas St.
Brackettville, TX 78832

Yldefonso Montalvo (1855–1941), also known by the name Obed Woods, built this dwelling about 1887. He used cedar pickets, caliche plaster, and other materials available in the area. Originally the kitchen and several outbuildings stood nearby. This is private property and not open to the public.

CARVER SCHOOL

302 W. Spring St.
Brackettville, TX 78832

A two-story, limestone building housed the only accredited school for African American and Black Seminole children between San Antonio and El Paso from 1914 and 1944. Later the building served as a meeting hall and cultural center for the community. Festivities held here included local Juneteenth celebrations and Seminole Day. Private property; not open to the public.

SEMINOLE INDIAN SCOUTS CEMETERY

RR 3348
Brackettville, TX 78832

Take Ranch Road 3348, which borders the west side of Fort Clark. Turn south at the light and go about 3 miles to the cemetery. Four Black Seminole Medal of Honor winners are buried here along with their comrades. Please respect this final resting place for many members of the Black Seminole community in Brackettville.

Four Medal of Honor winners are buried in this humble cemetery just outside Brackettville. Photo by author.

Restaurants

LAS MORAS GRILL

US 90, Fort Clark Springs, behind the Fort Clark Springs Pro Shop
Brackettville, TX 78832
830–422–3819
www.fortclark.com/las-moras-grill.html
Hours: Thursday–Monday, 11:00 a.m.–9:00 p.m.

Las Moras Grill has outdoor patio seating under huge trees overlooking Las Moras Creek. The restaurant serves reasonably priced burgers, salads, and full entrees such as crab-stuffed flounder and nacho chicken.

DARLA'S

US 90, across from entrance to Fort Clark Springs
Brackettville, TX 78832
Hours: open early most days for breakfast

Breakfast tacos, coffee, vegetarian and gluten-free items. If you stay at the Fort Clark Motel, this is the closest place for breakfast.

Darla's is a good place for breakfast in Brackettville. Photo by Thomas C. Self.

Lodging

FORT CLARK MOTEL

US 90, Fort Clark Springs
Brackettville, TX 78832
830–563–2493
www.fortclark.com/motel.html

Rates: weekdays, $60.00; weekends, $70.00

Pro-tip: Access to the fort, pool, and golf course is included.

Historic limestone cavalry barracks now used as a motel overlooks the nine-hole par 3 golf course. Each room has two queen beds, private bath, cable, and Wi-Fi. Handicapped rooms are available. Definitely a unique experience, but the motel could use some serious TLC.

An old army barracks serves as the motel's office at Fort Clark. Photo by Thomas C. Self.

Tent and RV Camping

FORT CLARK SPRINGS RV PARK

US 90, Fort Clark Springs
Brackettville, TX 78832
830–563–9340
www.fortclark.com/rv-park.html

Fees: $12.00 (tent site) or $23.50 (RV site) per night; additional charge for more than two people

Pro-tip: Campers have access to the pool, golf courses, and hiking trails. Call for camping reservations or email Rvpark@fortclark.com.

Tent camping with nearby showers is available for those who enjoy sleeping under the stars. Huge oak and pecan trees surround the area near Las Moras Creek. Barbecue facilities and picnic tables are located at each site. The RV campground is paved but has little shade. Long-term RV camping is also available. The park includes eighty-five RV spots with full hookups, cable, and Wi-Fi and fifteen tent sites.

Camp Wood

TX 55, 39 miles north of Uvalde

Population: 715

History

Camp Wood is located on the Nueces River. The area has been occupied for at least 4,000 years because of plentiful water and natural resources. Franciscans established Mission San Lorenzo de la Santa Cruz Mission in 1762 for the Lipan Apaches. In the nine years the mission was in operation, the Apaches helped build fourteen limestone and adobe buildings around a small plaza. In 1771, however, the Spanish burned the settlement and abandoned the mission policy. From 1857 to 1861 the US Army used the dilapidated site as a frontier outpost, Camp Wood.

After the Civil War, pioneer families came to the area. In 1920 Camp Wood became the northern terminus of the Uvalde and Northern Railroad, and the town site was formally laid out when workers from the Uvalde Cedar Company arrived. The post office was established in 1921, and the town was incorporated in 1936.

> **Charles Lindbergh's Unscheduled Stop**
>
> In March 1924 Charles A. Lindbergh made an unplanned stop in Camp Wood three years before his solo flight from New York to Paris. Lindbergh, then waiting to enter Brooks Field at San Antonio as a US Air Service cadet, was attempting to fly to California with a friend, Leon Klink, and followed the Uvalde and Northern Railroad up the Nueces River, mistaking it for the Southwestern Pacific along the Rio Grande. When the line ended at the recently established cedar town, Lindbergh, realizing his error, landed in a pasture to the north. Later, having flown to Camp Wood itself and landed on the main street, he attempted to take off, hit a telephone pole with a wing, and crashed into the paint section of Walter Pruett's hardware store. The two fliers remained in Camp Wood for several days, awaiting parts and making repairs.

Things to Do

The area offers swimming, fishing, kayaking, canoeing, floating down the Nueces River, camping, hiking, bird-watching, and hunting in season. Join the Old Settlers Reunion the first Saturday in August.

CAMP WOOD SWIMMING HOLE

River Rd., off TX 55
Camp Wood, TX

Pro-tip: There can be a strong current, so this is not for non-swimmers.

From Nueces Street (Texas 55), turn west onto W. 7th Street at the white limestone bank building across from the Camp Wood post office and go

Clear water invites swimmers and snorkelers near Camp Wood. Photo by Thomas C. Self.

about one mile down River Road. You will see a dirt parking area with a great view of the Nueces River. The water is about 15 feet deep at most and crystal-clear. Great for snorkelers, but beware the current.

Groceries

NUECES COUNTRY SMOKEHOUSE

1029 TX 55 South
Camp Wood, TX 78833
830–597–4242
Hours: Monday–Saturday, 10:00 a.m.–7:00 p.m.; Sunday, 10:00 a.m.–2:00 p.m.

This smokehouse also carries a small selection of grocery items, including ice cream, canned goods, chips, beer and wine, and ice. It also has deli items and meats to go. Sliced brisket with sweet, tangy sauce, chopped beef, and pulled pork come with a variety of sides. Also hot sandwiches and hamburgers.

Restaurants

CASA FALCON RESTAURANT

100 W. 2nd St.
Camp Wood, TX 78833
830–597–5111
Hours: sometimes closed if the fish are biting

Great breakfast buffet with biscuits and sausage gravy on top of everything else. The lunch buffet is somehow not as good, but the menu includes items like burgers and sandwiches. No credit cards accepted.

HARLEY'S HIDEAWAY BAR AND GRILL

500 E. 4th St. (RR 337)
Camp Wood, TX 78833
830–597–4223
Hours: none posted

Frozen margaritas, steaks. Bikers welcome.

Family-owned restaurants serve local favorites in Southwest Texas. Photo by Thomas C. Self.

TWO FAT BOYS BBQ

508 E. 4th St. (RR 337)
Camp Wood, TX 78833
830–987–6754 or
830–597–2333
www.twofatboysbbq.com
Hours: none posted

Tasty smoked barbecued ribs, turkey, and brisket. So-so sides. Bikers welcome.

MANUEL'S TACOS

TX 55
Camp Wood, TX 78833
Hours: Monday–Saturday, 7:00 a.m.–2:30 p.m.

Breakfast and lunch tacos, beer and wine.

Lodging

HILL COUNTRY MOTEL

200 E. 4th St.
Camp Wood, TX 78833
830–597–3278

Inexpensive motel accommodations with kitchenettes.

MILL WHEEL ON THE NUECES

TX 55
Camp Wood, TX 78833
830–597–4411
www.millwheelonthenueces.com

Cabins and guesthouses on private property right on the Nueces River. Great swimming hole!

NOW AND THEN COTTAGE

308 N. Frio St.
Camp Wood, TX 78833
830–591–3257 or 830–597–6195
www.nowandthencottage.com

Two quaint rock cottages located just minutes away from restaurants, grocery stores, and downtown shops. Only a short walk to the beautiful Nueces River.

WOODBINE INN

214 S. Nueces St.
Camp Wood, TX 78833
830–597–2310
www.nuecescanyonlodging.com

Motel accommodations in downtown Camp Wood featuring extra-long or queen-size beds.

Camping

BIG OAK RIVER CAMP
TX 55
Camp Wood, TX 78833
830–597–5280
www.bigoakrivercamp.com

Cabins as well as RV and tent camping with swimming pool. Shaded sites with beautiful pecan and oak trees. RV hookups with 20/30/50 amp service; concrete pull-through. Fully equipped log cabins. Picnic table, barbecue pit, and fire ring at all sites. Separate men's and women's bathhouses, camp store, ice, and laundry. Swimming, fishing, kayaking, tubing, and snorkeling.

WES COOKSEY RV PARK
TX 55, 3 miles south of town
Camp Wood, TX 78839
830–597–3223

Great place to camp and swim in the river! This Uvalde County park is on Lake Nueces and the Nueces River. Thirty RV hookups, all with water and electricity, some with sewer. Scuba, volleyball, boat ramp, basketball, showers, swimming, horseshoes. Tent camping and day use also available.

The Chihuahuan Desert has more varieties of cacti than any other place in the world. Photo by Thomas C. Self.

Comstock

US 90 and RR 163

Population: 223

Pro-tip: All vehicles are required to stop at the Border Patrol checkpoint a few miles east of Comstock on US 90. Be polite at all Border Patrol stations. It's not a joking matter. Yes, they have drug-sniffing dogs. This is a good place to use your cell phone, as service is spotty to nonexistent farther west.

History

The peaceful community of Comstock is located 24 miles northwest of Del Rio on US 90. The town was originally called Sotol City when it was first settled in 1883 with the coming of the railroad. The name was later changed to honor John Comstock, a railroad dispatcher. The Deaton Stage Line, which used a six-horse stagecoach to haul mail and other goods, also stopped in Comstock from 1888 to 1910.

Less than a mile from Comstock, a passenger train was stopped by furious gunfire from four outlaws in December 1896 as it neared Cow Creek. The outlaws managed to capture the train and tie up the crew. They stole money from a strongbox but couldn't open a large safe, which was left behind. They also took a package from the train that was addressed to one of the outlaws. Inside the package was his pocket watch, which had been sent to him after being repaired. The four were caught a week later by Texas Rangers.

Today the town is home to a US Border Patrol station that patrols 2,400 square miles, including 82 miles along the Rio Grande. The Shumla Archaeological Research and Education Center, a nonprofit rock art research center, is also headquartered here.

Restaurants and Supplies

QUICK STOP

US 90

Comstock, TX 78837

Gas is available 24/7 at the lone pump. Beer and ice are also available. Look for the fuel pump because the sign can easily be missed.

J AND P'S GRILL

US 90

Comstock, TX 78837

432–292–4338

Hours: Monday–Saturday, 11:00 a.m.–9:00 p.m.

Burgers, sandwiches, and a few entrees along with a full bar, cold beer, and wine. Unfortunately, J and P's is not open for breakfast. Try a Jello shot or J and P's specialty, a pickle shot. Yes, it's sour!

Lodging

COMSTOCK MOTEL

US 90

Comstock, TX 78837

432–292–4484

This small, locally owned and managed motel offers clean, basic rooms for about $65.00 per night.

Ranching and railroads brought prosperity to Southwest Texas. Photo by Thomas C. Self.

Concan

US 83, about 23.5 miles north of Uvalde

Population: 225

History

According to local lore, the town was named after "coon can," a Mexican card game. Though the site may have been settled as early as 1840, the first log cabin with a chimney was built here in the 1860s by Theophilus Watkins. The settlement was awarded a post office in 1880. The small town began to attract tourists in the 1920s. Today it is a popular spot for visitors to the Frio River and Garner State Park.

"Coon Can"

Conquian (also known as "cooncan," "coon can," and "coon-can") is generally regarded as the earliest form of rummy. A game for two players, conquian is played with a forty-card Spanish deck (a standard fifty-two-card deck with the 8's, 9's, and 10's removed can be used to form a forty-card deck), with the cards ranked from high to low: K-Q-J-7–6-5–4-3–2-A. To determine who deals first, the deck is shuffled and cut, and each player draws a card. The player drawing the lowest card deals first. Each player is dealt ten cards. The remaining cards are placed face down to form the stock. No upcard is turned.

The object of the game is to be the first to meld eleven cards, including the last card drawn. The non-dealer (called the "pone") begins by turning over the top card of the stack. He may either meld it immediately or discard it. If he melds it, he must discard from this hand. A distinctive feature of conquian is that drawn cards cannot be placed in a player's hand; they must be either melded immediately or discarded. Thereafter, each player in turn must either take the discard (and meld it immediately and discard another), or turn over the top of the stock and either meld it or discard it. A player may extend his existing melds or create new ones. A player may also "borrow" a card from one of his existing melds as long as the remaining cards form a valid meld.

If you decline a face card that could be added to one of your existing melds, your opponent may insist that you use the card. In so doing, he can force you to discard a card from your hand, probably one you were holding in reserve in hope of building a new meld. The game ends when one player melds his eleventh card. If the stock is exhausted with neither player having gone out, the game ends in a draw, and the stakes of the game are carried forward, to be claimed by whoever wins next.—*Thanks to Rummy-games.com*

Things to Do

The Frio River is a popular spot for swimming, snorkeling, tubing, kayaking, and canoeing. Canoe and tube rentals available at numerous outlets; tubes and kayaks are also for rent at Garner State Park. Tubes generally rent for $7.00 (without a bottom) to $10.00 (with bottom). Special tubes for ice chests are also available. Most outfitters, including those listed below, operate shuttles to and from river access points:

Andy's: 21488 TX 127, Concan, 830–232–5444, www.floatthefrio.com
Josh's Frio River Outfitters: US 83 at RR 127, Leakey and Concan, 830–232–6292, www.frioriveroutfitter.com
Happy Hollow Frio River Outfitters: 32580 US 83, Concan, 830–232–5266, www.onthefrio.com

Golfing, dancing to live music, horseback riding, and bat-viewing are other popular activities in this area.

THE CLUB AT CONCAN

520 Mountain Valley Dr. (CR 348), off TX 127
Concan, TX 78838
830–232–4471
www.concangolf.com
Hours: daylight to dusk
Fees: $20.00–$69.00

This is an eighteen-hole, 7,300-yard, par 72 championship course with pro shop, driving range, and grill. Please call for pricing, hours of operation, and specials. Memberships available. Lodging is also available.

RIVER OAKS MINIATURE GOLF

210 Encino Dr., one-half mile north of TX 127 via River Rd. (CR 648)
Concan, TX 78838
830–232–6106
www.frioriver.com
Hours: Daily, 9:00 a.m.–10:00 p.m. in summer; 10:00 a.m.–5:00 p.m. in off-season
Fee: $5.00 for 18 holes

There are two eighteen-hole courses and a large practice green, which is situated in a beautiful setting with plenty of benches. Great place for bird-watching, too.

FRIO BAT CAVE

RR 2690, southwest of Concan
888–502–9387
www.friobatflight.com
Hours: varies with season and sunset
Fee: $10.00–12.00 per person
Reservations: required in advance
Pro-tip: Dates and times change with the sunset, so call for tour times before you come! There is no tour if it's raining (because the bats don't fly in rainy weather) or if the roads are muddy or flooding.

Meet your guide at the gate, then drive about 2 miles on the ranch road to see the second-largest colony of Mexican free-tailed bats in the world. From March through October as many as 2–10 million bats emerge each evening from Frio Cave. Bats spend the winter in Mexico. Tours are for ten people minimum. No pets. Handicapped accessible.

JOE JIMMY'S

20970 TX 127
Concan, TX 78838
830–232–6118

Located next to Neal's Store. Live music, dancing under the stars, and summer concerts. Take dancing lessons on the large concrete dance slab or come in the fall to watch football.

Rattlin' Rodge

The self-declared mayor of Concan, Rattlin' Rodge, is a western diamondback rattlesnake that lives at Joe Jimmy's. You can watch him being fed by his handlers in the evenings. Of course, Rattlin' Rodge is not really the mayor of Concan—he lost by one vote. But everyone is too scared to tell him, or so the story goes.

HOUSE PASTURE

3064 CR 348 (River Rd.)
Concan, TX 78838
830–232–6580
www.housepasture.com
Hours: Gates open at 5:00 p.m.; concerts start at 9:00 p.m.
Admission: $10.00–20.00

Well-known musicians such as Gary P. Nunn, Kevin Fowler, Pat Green, and Whiskey Myers appear regularly at this popular spot. Tickets are available online. Outside seating. All ages welcome. Call for exact times. Casual attire.

ELM CREEK STABLES

US 83 near RR 1050
Concan, TX 78838
830–232–5365

Trail-riding horses for the whole family near the entrance of Garner State Park.

STABLES AT NEAL'S LODGES

20970 TX 127
Concan, TX 78838
830–232–6118
www.nealslodges.com.
Fee: $25.00 per person

Horseback riding for the family and hayrides in season. See the office in Neal's store.

Groceries and Supplies

B AND B GROCERY

83 RR 1050
Concan, TX 78838
830–232–6910

Restaurants

Some establishments may close during the winter. Call to confirm.

PATIO GRILLE AT THE CLUB AT CONCAN

520 Mountain Valley Dr. (CR 348), off TX 127
Concan, TX 78838
830–232–4251
www.clubatconcanconcangolf.com
Hours: Sunday–Thursday, 8:00 a.m.–3:00 p.m.; Friday and Saturday, 8:00 a.m.–5:00 p.m.

Breakfast tacos, burgers, sandwiches, soups, full bar. Happy hour 4:00 p.m.–7:00 p.m.

NEAL'S LODGES RESTAURANT

20970 TX 127
Concan, TX 78838
830–232–5813
www.nealsdiningroom.com
Hours: varies; check website

Generally open for breakfast, lunch, and dinner. Full breakfasts, nachos, burgers, sandwiches, chicken-fried steak. Outdoor seating overlooking the river. Closed the Monday after Thanksgiving until March 1 each year.

Rustic dining rooms serve Texas favorites like chicken-fried steak. Photo by Thomas C. Self.

HOUSE PASTURE CATTLE COMPANY
3064 CR 348 (River Rd.)
Concan, TX 78838
830–232–6580
www.housepasture.com
Hours: Tuesday–Sunday, 5:00 p.m.–10:00 p.m.

Steaks, grilled quail, burgers, sandwiches, appetizers, and full bar.

Lodging

Most prices per night are based on four-person occupancy. Most of these resorts offer cabins, tent camping, and RV sites. Bring your own linens, towels, dishes, and kitchen utensils unless confirmed otherwise by resort. Follow policies on pets and smoking. Cabins are often reserved up to a year in advance, so call for reservations before arrival. Also try the websites listed in chapter 1.

ANDY'S ON RIVER ROAD
US 83 and TX 127
Concan, TX 78838
830–232–5444
www.andysonriverroad.com

Cabins from $200.00 per night, motel-like suites from $150.00, and RV spots for $35.00. Tubes, kayaks, and shuttle available. Groceries and general store.

CAMP RIVER VIEW
1636 CR 350, 1.7 miles east of US 83
Concan, TX 78838
830–232–5412
www.friocampriverview.com

Sixteen two-bedroom, one-bath cabins. Kitchens, microwave, linens. Also RV park and tent camping. Groceries and tube rentals. Call for prices.

CLOUD DANCE LOG CABINS

Off CR 348 (River Rd.)
Concan, TX 78838
830–232–5994
www.clouddancecabins.com

Full kitchens, country furnishings, towels and linens furnished, satellite TV. Located on six acres one mile off River Road. Call for rates and policies.

CRIDER'S ON THE FRIO

US 83, 1.5 miles north of Garner State Park
Concan, TX 78838
830–232–5583
www.cridersonthefrio.com

Two-bedroom, three-bedroom, and four-bedroom cabins, some with fireplaces. From $200.00 to $650.00 per night; lower rates during the off-season. All cabins have heat and A/C and fully equipped kitchens with dishes and cookware. Each bed has a mattress pad, pillows, and spread. Bring your own sheets and blankets. Also bring towels and supplies for the washer, dryer, and dishwasher. General store and bakery located on site. Pet friendly. No tents or pop-ups allowed.

FRIO ACRES

1047 CR 350
Concan, TX 78838
830–232–4141
www.frioacres.com

Two four-bedroom lodges and five additional two-bedroom, two-bath cabins sleep up to eight people each. Cabins and lodges have large front porches, central heat and air conditioning, washer/dryer, and TVs with Direct TV. The fully equipped kitchens have coffee makers, microwaves, dishes, pots and pans, and utensils. Linens and towels are not provided. Outdoors you'll find picnic tables, barbecue grills and fire rings, and a volleyball net. Cabins are not handicap accessible. Small dogs are allowed. No smoking in cabins. No tent camping. Rates from $100.00 to $450.00 per night.

FRIO CANYON CABINS

32542 US 83, 1 mile north of Garner State Park
Concan, TX 78838
www.friocanyoncabins.com

Two large vacation houses and two duplexes on the Frio River. All have central air and heat, barbecue pits, full kitchens, and baths. Some have a washer/dryer and TV. Bring your own sheets and towels. Rates from $170.00 to $400.00 per night. Great views of the Frio River. No pets, no smoking.

FRIO COUNTRY RESORT

1801 CR 348 (River Rd.)
Concan, TX 78838
830–232–6625
www.friocountry.com

Thirty acres of private riverfront property. Cabins from $250.00 per night, vacation homes from $450.00, and RV spots from $35.00. No pets, no smoking.

MAGERS RIVER CAMP

2429 CR 350
Concan, TX 78838
830–232–5442
www.magersrivercamp.com

Tent camping, screen shelters, RV spots with full hookups, rental mobile trailers, and cabins at this family-owned and run property, which has been in business more than fifty years. Pets on leashes allowed. No smoking. Bring your own linens, dishes, and utensils. Located just across the Frio River from Garner State Park. The Magers family was one of the original owners of the land that became the state park, so their roots run deep.

NEAL'S LODGE

20970 TX 127
Concan, TX 78838
830–232–6118
www.nealslodges.com

Neal's has been in business since 1926, with seventy-one cabins, fifteen tent sites, and nine RV hookups near the river, plus twelve lodges in different areas of Concan and sixteen condos overlooking the Frio Canyon. The office is inside Neal's General Store. There is also a restaurant and music venue.

SEVEN BLUFF CABINS AND RV PARK

4251 CR 348 (River Rd.)
Concan, TX 78838
830–232–5260
www.7bluffcabins.com

Modern cabins, houses, RV sites as well as tubes and supplies. A clean, quiet place catering to families. Many guests have been coming every summer for twenty years or more. Quiet hours are from 10:00 p.m. to 8:00 a.m. No smoking. Pool, volleyball court, basketball court, river frontage. Pets are allowed, but see the website for the pet policies.

Del Rio

US 90 and US 277
Population: about 40,000
Pro-tip: If traveling west, fill up with gas and stock up on other essentials in Del Rio.

Del Rio was built around water, like this original irrigation canal from the 1870s. Photo by Thomas C. Self.

History

Water first drew human beings to this area thousands of years ago, but the first Europeans arrived in 1690 when the expedition of Spaniard Gaspar Castaño de Sosa crossed the Rio Grande near present-day Del Rio. In the 1700s a mission was settled across the river in Mexico by the Spanish. Then in 1856–57

San Felipe Springs became a stop on the 1,470-mile mail route from San Antonio to San Diego.

But perhaps the actual beginning of Del Rio occurred in 1868 when a group of entrepreneurs started the San Felipe Agricultural, Manufacturing, and Irrigation Company and paid employees in land instead of wages. A "Mother Ditch" irrigation canal had been dug in 1864 to provide water to a small, temporary settlement. Numerous canals, some dating to 1871, can still be seen in older parts of the city today.

The Galveston, Harrisburg and San Antonio Railroad, building from east to west, arrived in 1882. Two years later the first Southwestern train route across the United States was completed about 40 miles west of Del Rio.

A post office opened in 1883. The town of Del Rio was officially organized in 1905. New laws were soon passed that forbade horse racing in the streets, vagrancy, drunkenness, and nude swimming at San Felipe Springs. Val Verde officially became a county in 1885 and is 3,242 square miles in area, three times the size of Rhode Island.

To provide protection for the border during the Mexican Revolution (1910–20), the US Army established Camp Del Rio (later Camp Michie) as a semipermanent tent camp near what is today Moore Park (100 Swift Street). Troops stationed there primarily guarded railroad bridges to keep transportation routes open. A marker in Moore Park commemorates these events.

Pioneers left behind reminders like these antique bottles. Photo by Thomas C. Self.

Sunny weather brought Laughlin Air Force Base, home of the 47th Flying Training Wing, to Del Rio. The base began as Laughlin Army Air Field in 1943. When the Air Force was organized after World War II, the air force base was officially opened again in 1952. U-2 spy planes from Laughlin were among the first to provide photographic evidence of a Soviet missile installation during the Cuban missile crisis in 1962. Today T-6,

T-38, and T-1A aircraft are in the skies almost every day over Del Rio for pilot training for the US Air Force, Air Force Reserve, Air National Guard, and allied nation air forces.

The seat of Val Verde County, Del Rio is the largest city in Southwest Texas. Hotels, motels, restaurants, fast-food chains, and shopping centers of all kinds line Veteran's Boulevard (US 90). If you are traveling west to Big Bend or elsewhere from Del Rio, you are highly encouraged to purchase gas and other essentials here. The next town of any size is Alpine, approximately 200 miles away.

Places to Visit

DEL RIO/CIUDAD ACUÑA INTERNATIONAL BRIDGE

Junction of US 90, US 277, and US 277/377 at the Rio Grande

Pro-tip: If you cross the border, take your passport and be polite at all times. Don't go at night. Be safe.

There are no facilities on the Texas side of the river, but you can walk across the half-mile International Bridge to Del Rio's sister city, Ciudad Acuña, which has a city park that many people enjoy. Take a good look at the river as you walk across and have lunch in the park.

Ciudad Acuña, a city of about 150,000 in the state of Coahuila, is a center for manufacturing and international trade. Its history goes back to 1736, when the Spanish founded a short-lived mission near here. Mexican colonists settled the area in 1877. After several name changes,

> **The Carter Family**
>
> One of the most influential groups in country music history broadcast live twice a day in 1938–39 from radio station XERF, located in Ciudad Acuña. Partly because of this wide exposure, the Carter Family became the first real country music stars. They were the first group inducted into the Country Music Hall of Fame in 1970. Some of the songs they made famous include *The Wabash Cannonball*, *Wildwood Flower*, *Will the Circle Be Unbroken*, and their signature tune, *Keep on the Sunny Side*. The original group included A. P. Carter, his wife Sara, and his sister-in-law Maybelle. Later Maybelle and her daughters, Helen, June, and Anita, played together. June Carter became a famous country music star in her own right and married country music legend Johnny Cash.

the town was named Villa Acuña after poet Manuel Acuña in 1912. The town received the status of city (*ciudad*) from the Mexican government in 1951.

On January 9, 2014, the US State Department issued a travel warning to all US citizens to defer nonessential travel to the state of Coahuila, which continues to experience high rates of violent crimes, including kidnapping, armed carjacking, and narcotics-related murders. Of particular safety concern are casinos, sports bars, or other adult entertainment establishments, which US government personnel are not permitted to patronize.

Yet millions of US citizens safely visit Mexico each year for study, tourism, and business, including more than 150,000 who cross the border every day. The Mexican government dedicates substantial resources to protect visitors to major tourist destinations, and there is no evidence, according to the State Department, that criminal organizations have targeted US visitors or residents based on their nationality. Many people today travel to Mexico for medical care that is considerably less expensive than in the United States. A number of doctors, dentists, and pharmacies are located in Ciudad Acuña. The shopping and nightlife that attracted tourists twenty years ago have faded considerably, however.

LAUGHLIN HERITAGE FOUNDATION MUSEUM

309 S. Main
Del Rio, TX 78841
830–719–9380
Hours: Monday, Wednesday, Friday, and Saturday only, 10:00 a.m.–12:00 p.m. and 1:00 p.m.–4:00 p.m.

Photographs and memorabilia connected to Laughlin Air Force Base are on display, including artifacts related to the Cuban missile crisis of 1962.

Cuban Missile Crisis and the U-2 Spy Plane

An Air Force U-2 spy plane flown from Laughlin Air Force Base in Del Rio produced clear photographic evidence of medium-range and intermediate-range ballistic missile facilities in Cuba in September 1962, thus setting off the Cuban missile crisis. After thirteen days of tense negotiation between President John F. Kennedy and Premier Nikita Khrushchev of the Soviet Union, an agreement was reached to stand down. This was the closest the Cold War ever came to nuclear warfare.

WHITEHEAD MEMORIAL MUSEUM

1308 S. Main
Del Rio, TX 78840
830–774–7568
www.whiteheadmuseum.org
Hours: Tuesday through Saturday, 10:00 a.m.–6:00 p.m.; Sunday, 1–5 p.m.
Admission: adults $5.00, children $3.00

The history of Del Rio and Val Verde County is preserved at the Whitehead Memorial Museum. Nine historic buildings and more than two acres of beautifully landscaped grounds with a working windmill complete the museum space. The beautiful stone Perry Mercantile building dates to 1870. Be sure to go upstairs to see the Perry family living quarters. The museum has a wonderful collection of vintage farm machinery and old wine-making apparatus. Portions of the San Felipe irrigation canal of 1871 flow through the back of the museum's property. Kids of all ages will love the outdoor "Bang and Clang." Check with the museum for special programs for children and adults.

The Perry Mercantile Building at the Whitehead Memorial Museum dates to 1870. Photo by author.

VAL VERDE WINERY

100 Qualia Dr.
Del Rio, TX 78840
830–775–9714
www.valverdewinery.com
Hours: Monday–Saturday, 10:00 a.m.–5:00 p.m.

The Val Verde Winery makes small batch wines and award-winning olive oil. Photo by Thomas C. Self.

The Qualia family has been making wine in Del Rio since 1883, when Italian immigrant Frank Qualia received land from the San Felipe Agricultural, Manufacturing, and Irrigation Company. The family still makes small-batch, award-winning wines today using traditions passed on for generations. In addition to a wide variety of wines, they also produce high-quality olive oil from their own orchards. Tours and tastings are offered every day. Val Verde Winery is the oldest winery in continuous operation in Texas.

BRINKLEY MANSION

512 Qualia Dr.
Del Rio, TX 77840
Pro-tip: This is a private home. Do not trespass on private property.

A statue of Romulus and Remus of Roman myth graces the grounds of the Brinkley Mansion. Photo by Thomas C. Self.

If you're going to the Val Verde Winery, you should drive by this Spanish eclectic-style mansion a few doors down. The original part of the home was built between 1931 and 1934 by the Brinkley family and at one time included lush grounds with over 8,000 rose bushes and two lighted fountains. At night the house was lit with colored lights, and music was piped outdoors along the fence. Stories are that people used to come at night to dance and take in the show.

The house was built by Dr. John R. Brinkley, who experimented with transplanting goat glands into male patients to cure them of impotence while living in Kansas. He even ran for governor of Kansas twice, but he moved to Del Rio in 1931 when he lost his medical license. Dr. Brinkley owned a number of radio stations in his life, but also lost his radio license in the United States. He opened the powerful XER radio station in Ciudad Acuña in 1931 to escape US radio restrictions.

Border Radio

In 1931 Dr. J. R. Brinkley of Del Rio opened radio station XER (later known as XERA and XERF) at 840 on the AM dial in Ciudad Acuña. Known as the "Border Blaster" at 150,000 watts, XER was so powerful it could be heard all the way to Kansas by 1932. Local ranchers near Del Rio reported they could hear the radio in their wire fence lines.

The station had the most powerful signal in North America by the 1960s at 250,000 watts. Unfortunately, little remains of the old radio station, but the Brinkley Mansion in Del Rio still serves up the memories.

MASON-FOSTER HOUSE

123 Hudson St.
Del Rio, TX 77840
Pro-tip: This is a private home. Do not trespass on private property.
This historic home was built around 1888. A spring on the property was once used for mineral baths and a medicinal drink.

The Mason-Foster House reminds us of the wealth that was here in the 1880s. Photo by Thomas C. Self.

TAYLOR-RIVERS HOUSE

100 Hudson Dr.
Del Rio, TX 78840

Pro-tip: This is a private home. Do not trespass on private property.
Frank Taylor and his wife Paula, original settlers of Del Rio, moved here about 1870 and built this one-story adobe residence. Paula later married Charles Rivers and donated land for a school and a cemetery.

GLENN-DOWE HOUSE

Corner of Garfield and Washington Streets
Del Rio, TX 77840

This historic home was built in 1901 and is now used for commercial purposes.

The Glenn-Dowe House is a fine example of a Victorian gingerbread cottage. Photo by Thomas C. Self.

SAN FELIPE LION'S PARK, BLUE HOLE PARK, HORSESHOE PARK, ROTARY PARK

Off US 90 East near 277, and various locations through town
Del Rio, TX 78840
830–774–8454

San Felipe Creek runs through the San Felipe Country Club and a series of city parks. There are several great swimming holes with hard limestone bottoms and stone banks, shaded by pecan and elm trees in the parks. The clear pools are shallow enough for children and long enough to swim short laps. US 90 E is nearby. A paved trail known as the San Felipe Creekway is about a mile long and connects Horseshoe Park and Lion's Park.

GEORGE PAUL MEMORIAL BULLRIDING SUPERBULL

Val Verde County Fairgrounds
2006 N. Main St.
Del Rio, TX 78440
830–775–9595
www.georgepaulmemorialbullriding.com
Admission: $20.00

George Paul Memorial Bullriding Superbull takes place in Del Rio annually during the last weekend in April at the Val Verde County Fairgrounds. This is the largest bull-riding event in the United States, drawing participants from all over the country. The arena even has a Jumbotron for instant replays.

The Superbull event is named in memory of George Paul, who was born and grew up in Del Rio. Watch some of the finest bull riders, steer ropers, barrel racers, and bucking broncos in the world. Rodeo clowns, a children's calf chase, and rock and roll round out the weekend.

The action is fast and furious at the Del Rio bull-riding event in April. Photo by Todd Brewer.

Wolfman Jack

Wolfman Jack became the most famous disc jockey in the United States during the 1960s. He joined border blaster radio XERF-FM in Ciudad Acuña in 1962. His growling style could be heard coast to coast, thanks to high broadcast power and syndication. Wolfman Jack was heard on more than 2,000 radio stations in fifty-three countries at his peak. He helped popularize rock and roll and many black artists with his programming. Wolfman Jack's real name was Robert Weston Smith (1938–95). He left XERF after a shootout at the station left two people dead in 1964. His gravely voice reminded listeners of the great bluesman Howlin' Wolf.

Groceries

H-E-B SUPERMARKET AND PHARMACY

200 Veteran's Blvd.
Del Rio, TX 78840
830–768–3617

Hours: Daily, 6:00 a.m.–midnight; pharmacy: 8:30 a.m.–8:30 p.m. (may vary)

Located near the intersection of US 90 and US 277, this is the place to load up on wonderful Mexican pastries for the road in addition to food of every description.

WALMART SUPERCENTER

2410 Dodson Ave. (just off Veteran's Blvd.)
Del Rio, TX 78840
830–775–687

Hours: Daily 24 hours; pharmacy, 9:00 a.m. – 9:00 p.m. (may vary)

In addition to a large grocery section, this is the place to pick up anything you may have forgotten for your trip: camping gear, automotive supplies, clothing, the kitchen sink.

Restaurants

For those seeking local flavor, there are a number of independently owned restaurants in Del Rio. There are also many chain restaurants along US 90 (Veteran's Boulevard) in Del Rio that are not listed here. This guide does not rate any commercial establishment.

THE BROWN BAG

440 S. Main
830–768–4837
Del Rio, TX 78840

Hours: Monday–Friday, 9:00 a.m.–3:30 p.m.; Saturday 11:00 a.m.–3:00 p.m.

This deli is located in a historic building downtown and serves a variety of sandwiches, salads, tortilla soup, fish tacos, and other items. Excellent food and good service.

CHINTO'S SUPER TACO MEXICAN RESTAURANT

400 E. 6th
Del Rio, TX 78840
830–774–1592
Hours: Daily, 6:00 a.m.–2:30 p.m.

This small family-run place serves breakfast tacos, homemade tortillas, and more.

CRIPPLE CREEK STEAKHOUSE

5667 US 90 W
Del Rio, TX 78840
830–775–0153
www.cripplecreeksteakhouse.com
Hours: Monday–Thursday, 5:00 p.m.–10:00 p.m.; Friday and Saturday, 5:00 p.m.–11:00 p.m.

Serving prime rib, grilled mesquite steaks, and seafood. Try the Hunter's Combo with a 9-ounce grilled sirloin and grilled quail for $19.95 or the Sportman's Platter for $25.95, with jumbo shrimp, quail, frog legs, and catfish. Have a cucumber margarita or your favorite drink from the full bar. Easy to spot just west of Del Rio on US 90, as it is the only log cabin in Val Verde County.

ICON BAR AND GRILL

11207 US 90 W
Del Rio, TX 78840
830–775–8591
Hours: Thursday–Saturday, 5:00 p.m.–10:00 p.m.

This restaurant takes advantage of its location at the Amistad Lake Resort with a beautiful outdoor patio overlooking the lake. Full bar, steak, seafood, pasta, burgers, and a large appetizer menu. Try the Ahi Tuna or Corona Chicken.

JITRA THAI CUISINE

904 E. Gibbs St. (US 90 E toward Brackettville)
Del Rio, TX 78840
830–775–7553
Hours: Daily, 10:00 a.m.–9:00 p.m.

Try one of the curries or the Tom Yum Gai soup. Also serves many Chinese dishes.

MANUEL'S STEAKHOUSE

1312 Veteran's Blvd.
Del Rio, TX 78840
830–488–6044
Hours: Daily, 11:00 a.m.–11:00 p.m.

A favorite restaurant in Ciudad Acuña has moved across the border, serving Mexican food and steaks. Try the Rough Canyon plate with bacon-wrapped shrimp, grilled shrimp, and frog legs.

MEMO'S RESTAURANT

804 E. Losoya
Del Rio, TX 78840
830–774–1583
www.memosrestaurant.com
Hours: Monday–Saturday, 11:00 a.m.–2:00 p.m., 5:30 p.m.–9:30 p.m.

Open since 1936, this local favorite serves fajitas, enchiladas, burgers, and more in a creekside setting. Occasional live music.

RIVER CITY DOUGHNUT AND COFFEE HOUSE

500 Veteran's Blvd.
Del Rio, TX 78840
830–775–8769
Hours: Saturday–Wednesday, 8:00 a.m.–12:00 p.m.; Thursday, 7:00 a.m.–12:00 p.m.; Friday, 6:00 a.m.–12:00 p.m.

Freshly made donuts and croissants at this family-run place. Drive-through window.

WRIGHT'S STEAKHOUSE

8116 US 90 W
Del Rio, TX 78840
830–775–2621
Hours: Tuesday–Sunday, 5:00 p.m.–9:00 p.m.

Wright's is located about 8 miles west of Del Rio on the south side of the highway. It is set back and has a large parking lot in front, although the sign itself can be missed. Try the 16-ounce garlic-crusted rib eye and the onion rings. One order of freshly made onion rings is enough for the whole table!

Chicken-fried steak is another popular choice. The salad bar and veggies are basic, but the full bar makes up for it. Be sure to check out the Christmas tree decorated for each change of season and the occasional live music.

Lodging

Most motels in Del Rio are located on Veteran's Boulevard, as US 90 is known in town. This guide does not rate any commercial establishments, and there are many other accommodations that are not listed here. If you're tired after a long drive, however, these motels are pretty reliable. The next town with much in the way of lodging options is Alpine, about 200 miles west.

BEST WESTERN INN

810 Veteran's Blvd.
Del Rio, TX 78840
830–775–7511 or 800–336–353

Standard motel with business center, outdoor pool, complimentary breakfast, guest laundry, cable TV with HBO, and free Wi-Fi.

Southwest Texas opens many doors to adventure for travelers. Photo by Thomas C. Self.

HAMPTON INN

2219 Bedell Ave.
Del Rio, TX 78840
830–775–9700

Located one block off of Veteran's Boulevard. Standard motel with pool, fitness room, guest laundry, business center, and free breakfast.

HOLIDAY INN

2410 Bedell Ave.
Del Rio, TX 78840
830–774–7774 (front desk); 800–315–2621 (reservations)

Ninety-three smoke-free rooms with outdoor pool, fitness center, business center, free Wi-Fi, and free breakfast. Located one block off Veteran's Boulevard.

LA QUINTA INN

2005 Veteran's Blvd.
Del Rio, TX 78840
830–775–7591

Standard motel with pool, guest laundry, free Wi-Fi, free breakfast.

MOTEL 6

2115 Veteran's Blvd.
Del Rio, TX 78840
830–774–2115

Free morning coffee, a year-round outdoor pool, and a coin laundry as well as free Wi-Fi.

QUALITY INN

3616 Veteran's Blvd.
Del Rio, TX 78840
830–775–2933

Standard motel with free Wi-Fi, business center, guest laundry, pool, fitness center, and free breakfast. Smoking rooms are available, but no pets are allowed.

RAMADA INN

2101 Veteran's Blvd.
Del Rio, TX 78840
830–775–1511

Two heated pools (one with a great waterfall), fitness room, free Wi-Fi, cable TV, business center, laundry, and room service. Restaurant and full bar on site. Pet friendly.

WHISPERING PALMS INN

1300 Veteran's Blvd.
Del Rio, TX 78840
830–488–6270

Pool, free Wi-Fi, bar and restaurant, boat parking, microwave, and mini-fridge, pet friendly. Can arrange fishing guide service. Complimentary coffee in the morning.

RV Parks

AMERICAN CAMPGROUND

10348 US 90 W
Del Rio, TX 78840
830–775–6484

Pool, playground, Wi-Fi and cable, laundry, showers, recreation hall. Also cabin rentals. Located directly across from the Black Brush Point boat launch. Eighty-five sites.

BROKE MILL RV PARK

6069 US 90 W
Del Rio, TX 78840
830–422–2961
www.brokemillrvpark.com

Swimming pool, laundry, showers, Wi-Fi, fitness center. Pet friendly. Barbecue with live music every Thursday evening.

HIDDEN VALLEY RV PARK

341 Bolner Lane
Del Rio, TX 78840
830–775–0045
www.hiddenvalleydelrio.com

Located off South Main in a historic neighborhood of Del Rio, this park has plenty of shade for your RV. Most sites have picnic tables. Free Wi-Fi and cable, fitness center, laundry, pet friendly.

HOLIDAY TRAV-L-PARK

11490 US 90 W, about 10 miles west of Del Rio
Del Rio, TX 78840
830–775–7275 or 800–545–2364 (reservations)

Pool, playground, laundry, cable and Wi-Fi, showers, some shade.

LONESOME DOVE RV PARK

4832 US 90
Del Rio, TX 78840
830–774–1823

Laundry, showers, Wi-Fi, pet friendly, tent camping. Fifty-four sites.

THREE RIVERS RV PARK

US 90 W, about 8 miles west of Del Rio
Del Rio, TX 78840
830–778–2241

Wi-Fi and cable, showers, laundry, pet friendly.

Lodging for Lake Amistad

THE ANGLER'S LODGE

8969 US 90 W
Del Rio, TX 78840
830–775–1586
www.theanglerslodge.com

All rooms have two queen beds, and some have kitchenettes. The cafe is open from 5:00 a.m. to 8:00 p.m. or later on fishing tournament weekends. Visit the tackle store and try some of their original baits. Pet friendly.

AMISTAD LAKE RESORT

11207 US 90 W
Del Rio, TX 78840
830–775–8591 or 800–775–8591
www.amistadlakeresort.com

Enjoy the swimming pool and the view of Lake Amistad at this pet-friendly motel with forty rooms that include mini-fridge, microwave, and free Wi-Fi.

LAKE AMISTAD RENTALS

830–775–8779
www.lakeamistadrentals.com

Condos, mobile homes, cabins, cabanas, and RV spots are available in various locations around the lake. No pets allowed. Rates vary.

HILLCREST LODGE

100 Hillcrest Road
Del Rio, TX 78840
401–996–9542
www.texaslodge.net

A three-bedroom, 2.5-bath house overlooking Lake Amistad. Pool table, outdoor barbecue grill, full kitchen, washer and dryer, AC, cable TV and Wi-Fi.

RIVER STREET LODGING

830–734–3248
www.riverstlodgingandrv.yolasite.com

Mobile homes and cabins on Lake Amistad. Parking for boats. Rates vary.

RUTHIE'S RENTALS

830–774–5377
www.ruthiesrentals.com

Mobile homes for rent near Lake Amistad. Rates vary.

April and May are the best months to see blooming cactus in the Lower Pecos Canyonlands. Photo by Thomas C. Self.

Eagle Pass

US 277 and US 57

Population: 26,255

Eagle Pass is the home of interesting history and the only gambling casino in Texas, so it's certainly worth a visit.

History

During the Mexican War of 1846 a company of Texas Mounted Volunteers under the command of Capt. John A. Veatch established an observation post on the Rio Grande beside an old smuggler's trail that crossed the river where Eagle Pass is located today. The crossing, known as El Paso del Águila, was so named because of frequent flights by Mexican eagles near the river. In 1849 Fort Duncan was established by the US Army two miles upstream, and a small settlement began. John Twohig surveyed the site in 1850 and named it Eagle Pass. A stage line between Eagle Pass and San Antonio was established in 1851. Our Lady of Refuge Catholic Church was constructed in 1852.

The settlement and adjoining fort were frequently attacked by the Lipan Apache and Comanche Indians during those years. Piedras Negras, established in 1850 across from Eagle Pass in Mexico, became a haven for fugitive slaves from the United States, and both banks of the river were infested with outlaws. In 1855 James H. Callahan crossed into Mexico at Eagle Pass with three companies of volunteer rangers in pursuit of Lipans and Kickapoos. After a fight with Mexican forces, he fell back on Piedras Negras and set the village afire as he crossed back into Eagle Pass.

During the Civil War, a party of renegades crossed from Piedras Negras and overran the Confederate garrison at Fort Duncan. The townsmen, fighting from behind a barricade of cotton bales, successfully drove off their assailants. Following federal occupation of Brownsville in 1863, Eagle Pass became an important shipment point for Confederate cotton. After the war the last Confederate force in the field, the Shelby expedition, crossed the Rio Grande at Eagle Pass and buried the last flag to fly over Confederate troops in the river.

Maverick County was organized in 1871, and Eagle Pass became the county seat. In 1882 the Galveston, Harrisburg and San Antonio Railway connected the isolated community to the rest of the country. Rail construction continued into Mexico at Piedras Negras as the Mexican National

Railway, and the community became an important international center.

By 1987, five industrial plants, or maquiladoras, were located in Eagle Pass and nineteen in Piedras Negras. Textile and arms manufacturing were the leading employers. Significant oil finds have boosted the economy in recent years.

Places to Visit

FORT DUNCAN

For information about Fort Duncan and the Fort Duncan Museum, see the chapter on forts.

KICKAPOO LUCKY EAGLE CASINO

794 Lucky Eagle Drive
Eagle Pass, TX 78852
888–255–8259
www.luckyeagletexas.com

Welcome to the only casino in Texas! Owned by the Kickapoo Indians, there is plenty of electronic gaming, Texas hold 'em, seven-card stud, and bingo to keep you on your toes. The casino features four bars, four restaurants,

The only casino in Texas draws gaming fans from the United States and Mexico. Courtesy Kickapoo Lucky Eagle Casino.

live entertainment Thursdays through Saturdays in the lounge, a Tejano music showcase on Sundays, and a hotel.

The Kickapoo, an Algonquian-speaking group of fewer than 1,000 individuals scattered across Texas, Oklahoma, Kansas, and northern Mexico, are the remnants of a larger tribe that once lived in the central Great Lakes region. The small, private Kickapoo Indian Reservation of Texas is located just south of Eagle Pass as a community of less than 420 persons. Another group of Kickapoo live most of the year at El Nacimiento, Mexico, about 130 miles southwest of Eagle Pass. The Kickapoo strive to maintain their traditional culture, from religion to home construction to language and education. They take kinship obligations and communal responsibilities very seriously and are reluctant to act in ways contrary to tradition. They refer to themselves as Mexican Kickapoo and have dual citizenship in both countries. They do not encourage visitors at the reservation. Visit the casino instead.

PIEDRAS NEGRAS, COAHUILA, MEXICO

Pro-tip: Passport required if you cross the border. Be polite at all times. Don't go at night. Be safe.

Piedras Negras, a city of about 150,000, lies at the northeastern edge of Coahuila on the US-Mexico border, across the Río Bravo (Rio Grande) from Eagle Pass. The Eagle Pass–Piedras Negras International Bridge, Camino Real International Bridge, and the Eagle Pass Union Pacific International Railroad Bridge connect the two countries.

Piedras Negras was founded in 1849. In 1855, the town was looted by a small force of 130 Texans that had been organized by Texas slaveholders for a punitive expedition against a nearby border settlement of fugitive slaves and Indians.

In Spanish Piedras Negras means "black stones," a reference to the area's coal deposits. After the discovery of huge deposits of coal in the region and the construction of a railroad track in 1883, the regional economy flourished; on December 1, 1888, the town was granted city status and named Ciudad Porfirio Díaz, who was then president of Mexico. After the fall of Díaz during the Mexican Revolution in 1911, the city reverted to the name Piedras Negras. Coal was formerly mined on the US side near Eagle Pass, but this mine closed around 1905 after a fire. Mexico currently operates two large coal-fired power plants 30 miles south of Piedras Negras.

The 1993 movie *Like Water for Chocolate* was filmed in the area around Piedras Negras. On April 24, 2007, an F4 tornado struck the city, killing three people there and seven in Eagle Pass.

As of May 2015, the US State Department was warning travelers against visiting the state of Coahuila. Violence and criminal activity continue to be high along the border between Piedras Negras and Nuevo Laredo. Murder, kidnapping, and armed carjacking have been reported. Of particular safety concern are casinos, sports bars, or other adult entertainment establishments.

Many people today travel to Mexico for medical care, which is considerably less expensive than in the United States. A number of doctors, dentists, and pharmacies are located in Piedras Negras. The shopping and nightlife that attracted tourists twenty years ago have faded considerably.

Groceries

H-E-B SUPERMARKET AND PHARMACY

2135 E. Main St.
Eagle Pass, TX 78852
830–773–03345
Hours: Daily, 6:00 a.m.–midnight; pharmacy: 8:00 a.m.–8:00 p.m.

Fruits, veggies, meats, bakery, and all sorts of packaged food items you may need on your trip. Don't forget sunglasses and sunscreen!

WALMART SUPERCENTER

96 S. Bibb Ave.
Eagle Pass, TX 78852
830–773–9403
Hours: Daily, 24 hours

In addition to a large grocery section, this is the place to pick up anything you may have forgotten for your trip, such as camping gear, automotive supplies, clothing, and electronics.

Pull up a chair and sit a spell. Dining is relaxed in Southwest Texas. Photo by Thomas C. Self.

Restaurants

There are plenty of places to eat and stay in Eagle Pass that are not mentioned here. This guide presents only a sampling and does not rate any commercial establishment.

SAGE STEAKHOUSE

Lucky Eagle Casino
794 Lucky Eagle Dr.
Eagle Pass, TX 78852
888–255–8259
www.luckyeagletexas.com
Hours: Thursday–Sunday, 5:00 p.m.–11:00 p.m.
Pro-tip: Reservations are recommended.

Delicious, aged Angus beef and fine wine make any day even better. Try the chorizo-stuffed shrimp for $10.99 or the pan-seared fois gras for $17.99 as starters. Several lovely salads are available as well as French onion soup. Your choice of entrees includes a Kobe beef burger for $14.99, Chilean sea bass for $27.99, or a 21-ounce Porterhouse steak for $39.99.

MEZQUITE CAFE

Lucky Eagle Casino
794 Lucky Eagle Dr.
Eagle Pass, TX 78852
888–255–8259
www.luckyeagletexas.com

Hours: Sunday–Thursday, 7:00 a.m.–2:00 p.m., 5:00 p.m.–9:00 p.m.; Friday and Saturday, 7:00 a.m.–2:00 p.m., 5:00 p.m.–10:00 p.m.

The hotel's casual dining spot for breakfast, lunch, and dinner. The casino and hotel also have a traditional casino buffet and small cafe available for players.

PARRILLA DE SAN MIGUEL

408 S. Texas Dr.
Eagle Pass, TX 78852
830–757–3100
www.parrilladesanmiguel.com

Hours: Daily, 11:00 a.m.–11:00 p.m.

Huge menu with steaks, seafood, Mexican dishes, burgers, and more. Try one of the four versions of sautéed mushroom appetizers or the grilled panela cheese. Entrées include steak and shrimp combos and mahimahi topped with shrimp. Full bar. Service can be spotty.

JADE PALACE

2076 N. Veterans Blvd., Suite A
Eagle Pass, TX 78852
830–752–1661
www.jadepalaceeaglepass.com

Hours: Monday–Saturday, 11:00 a.m.–9:00 p.m.

Spicy mofu tofu, teriyaki chicken, chicken curry, pork with garlic sauce, and vegetable lo mein are just a sample of the items on the moderately priced menu at the Jade Palace. Good Chinese food is rare in Southwest Texas, making this little spot a delicious find.

HUDDLE HOUSE

2352 El Indio Hwy. (RR 1021)
Eagle Pass, TX 78852
830–776–7083
Hours: Daily, 24 hours

Good all-day breakfast place with French toast and generous egg platters. Burgers, salads, and traditional entrées like chicken-fried steak.

Lodging

LUCKY EAGLE HOTEL

768 Lucky Eagle Dr.
Eagle Pass, TX 78852
830–773–2255
www.luckyeagletexas.com

The hotel adjoining the Kickapoo Lucky Eagle Casino has 249 well-appointed rooms with free Wi-Fi, cable, and refrigerators. Rooms range from standard king and queen rooms to suites with dining and sitting areas. Swimming pool and fitness center.

HAMPTON INN EAGLE PASS

3301 E. Main St.
Eagle Pass, TX 78852
830–757–5565

Standard motel with pool, fitness room, guest laundry, business center, and free breakfast. No smoking, no pets—service animals only.

TOWNEPLACE SUITES BY MARRIOT

2033 N. Veterans Blvd.
Eagle Pass, TX 78852
830–757–0077
www.marriott.com/hotels/travel/egpts-towneplace-suites-eagle-pass/

Heated outdoor pool, fitness center, fully equipped kitchens in all rooms, microwaves, refrigerators, Wi-Fi, cable, and free breakfast. No smoking. Pet friendly.

LA QUINTA

2525 East Main St.
Eagle Pass, TX 78852
830–773–7000
www.laquintaeaglepass.com

Range of rooms available. Business center, guest laundry, outdoor pool, free Wi-Fi and cable, free breakfast. Pet friendly.

HOLIDAY INN EXPRESS

2007 Veterans Blvd.
Eagle Pass, TX 78852
830–757–3050
www.hiexpress.com

Fitness center, hot tub, swimming pool, free breakfast, free Wi-Fi and cable, microwaves and refrigerators. No pets. No smoking.

MICROTEL INN & SUITES

2352 El Indio Hwy. (RR 1021)
Eagle Pass, TX 78852
830–776–5661
www.microtelinn.com

Standard motel with free continental breakfast, pool, Wi-Fi and cable. No pets. No smoking.

MOTEL 6

2338 E Main St.
Brackettville, TX 78852
830–757–8100
www.motel6.com/en/motels.tx.eagle-pass

This unpretentious budget lodging is off US 277, 1.6 miles from the International Center for Trade and 9.4 miles from the Kickapoo Lucky Eagle Casino.

The ranchland can be as forbidding as this thorny agarita near the Mexican border. Photo by author.

El Indio

RR 1021 (El Indio Hwy.), 17 miles south of Eagle Pass

Population: 263

A large ranch was established here in the 1850s. It is likely that Mexican revolutionary Francisco Madero launched his revolution against the regime of Porfirio Díaz from the Indio Ranch sometime in 1910. Incidents of cattle thieving, gun running, and military operations took place in and around the area throughout the Mexican Revolution (1910–20).

Leakey

US 83, about 40 miles north of Uvalde

Population: 387

History

After thousands of years of occupation by various Native American groups, Anglo settlers first arrived here in 1856. A small community began with a post office in 1883. When Real County was organized in 1913, Leakey (LAY-key) was made the county seat, although the town was not incorporated until 1951. Although lumbering, freighting, and cultivating cotton and corn were initially important to the local economy, these activities were eventually superseded by ranching, and in particular the raising of Angora goats; tourism also provides an increasingly significant source of revenue.

The town of Leakey welcomes visitors to the Western Hill Country. Photo by Thomas C. Self.

About 5 miles south of Leakey, US 83 nears one of the local cattle trails in Texas that converged with the legendary Chisholm Trail in the 1870s and 1880s. Thousands of longhorns were driven to northern markets during the first years after the Civil War. Many local settlers took part in the drives, which lasted for months. At times, the trail was used by herds of 200–300 hogs being driven 40 miles to local markets as well. The cattle industry grew rapidly after the Civil War and revived the depressed Texas economy.

The McLaurin Raid

The last Indian raid in Frio Canyon occurred on April 19, 1881, about 5 miles northwest of US 83 near Ranch Road 336. John McLaurin was away when his wife, Kate Ringer McLaurin, her three small children, and Allen Lease were attacked by Lipan Apaches. Kate and the children were in the garden when the Indians rode up to plunder the home, possibly looking for food. Allen, age fourteen, thought the pigs had gotten into the house and went to investigate the noise. The attackers shot and killed him. Catherine was also shot and died hours later, but the young children were unharmed. Maud, age six, ran for help. Neighbors gave chase for 70 miles before soldiers from Fort Clark took command. Soldiers trailed the Apaches into Mexico, reportedly killing all but two.

Places to Visit

WILDLIFE ART MUSEUM

RR 337, 3 blocks east of US 83
Leakey, TX 78873
830–232–5607
Hours: Monday–Saturday, 9:00 a.m.–5:00 p.m.

Features the art of taxidermy, sculpture, paintings, and carvings.

REAL COUNTRY HISTORICAL MUSEUM

Evergreen St., one-half block north of the Real County Courthouse
Leakey, TX 78873
830–232–5330
www.realcountyhistoricalmuseum.com
Hours: Friday and Saturday, 10:00 a.m.–4:00 p.m.
Admission: $1.00 for adults, $0.50 for children

Exhibits on the history and heritage of Real County show how the pioneers lived.

Things to Do

Popular activities are swimming, fishing, kayaking, canoeing, floating down the Frio River, camping, hiking, bird-watching, and hunting in season. Lots of motorcycle and car clubs love to ride to Leakey as well.

Groceries

LEAKEY MERCANTILE

417 US 83
Leakey, TX 78873
830–232–6299
Hours: Monday–Thursday, 7:00 a.m.–7:00 p.m.; Friday, 7:00 a.m.–8:00 p.m.; Saturday, 8:00 a.m.–8:00 p.m.; Sunday, 10:00 a.m.–5:00 p.m.

Fresh produce, meat, camping supplies, beer and wine.

Restaurants

BENT RIM GRILL

RR 337, one-half mile west of US 83
Leakey, TX 78873
830–232–6649
www.bentrimgrill.com

Hours: Monday–Thursday, 10:00 a.m.–5:00 p.m.; Friday–Saturday, 8:00 a.m.–6:00 p.m.; Sunday, 8:00 a.m.–5:00 p.m.

Try the Texas Toothpicks, which are slivers of onion and jalapeño peppers, battered and fried. Or maybe you'd prefer the sweet potato waffle fries, chili cheese fries, or fried dill pickle spears. Also serving amazing burgers and dogs. Bikers welcome. Next door is the Frio Canyon Motorcycle Stop, where you can get your Twisted Sisters T-shirts.

BUCKHORN BAR AND GRILL

4347 US 83 south
Leakey, TX 78873
830–232–4755
www.thebuckhornbarandgrill.com

Hours: Tuesday–Thursday, 11:00 a.m.–10:00 p.m.; Friday, 11:00 a.m.–12:00 a.m.; Saturday, 11:00 a.m.–1:00 a.m.; Sunday, 12:00 p.m.–8:00 p.m.

Ride the mechanical bull, sing karaoke, or dance to a live band on Saturday nights. You can also play traditional Texas games like horseshoes and washers. Try some appetizers like bacon bombers, bloomin' onions, or bottle caps before ordering up your burger. Salads and children's plates are also on the menu. Adults can wash it all down with good, cold beer.

THE HOG PEN GRILL

373 US 83 at RR 337
Leakey, TX 78873
830–232–4868 or 830–279–8408
www.thehogpenstore.com

Hours: Thursday–Monday, 10:00 a.m.–11:30 p.m.

Grab some traditional Texas barbecue, including beef brisket, sausage links, ribs, smoked chicken or boudain. Served with baked beans, potato salad, pickles, onions, fresh sliced bread, and ice-cold beer. Bikers welcome. Generally open normal business hours, but sometimes not.

Bikers are always welcome for beer and barbecue. Photo by Thomas C. Self.

MAMA CHOLE'S

US 83 downtown
Leakey, TX 78873
830–232–6111
Hours: Daily, 11:00 a.m.–9:00 p.m.

This small family-owned Tex-Mex restaurant serves good enchiladas, chicken-fried steak, chicken fajita salad, and burgers.

MILL CREEK CAFE

859 US 83
Leakey, TX 78873
830–233–4805
Hours: Daily, 7:00 a.m.–9:00 p.m.

Good breakfast buffet, as well as burgers, sandwiches, chicken-fried steak, catfish, and more.

CHICKEN EARL'S

703 US 83 at the Pecan Farm
Leakey, TX 78873
830–232–5001
Hours: Tuesdays only, 11:00 a.m.–7:00 p.m.

Great fried chicken with mashed potatoes, green beans, and pinto beans. Many people make this spot a Tuesday tradition.

Lodging

Since many vacation cabins are rented months in advance, plan to make your reservations early. Also see the websites listed in chapter 1.

CAMP LIVE OAK

1650 US 83
Leakey, TX 78873
830–232–4152
www.campliveoak.com

Eight cabins on the Frio River, just 1.7 miles north of the Leakey courthouse. All cabins have heat and air, ceiling fans, full kitchens with dishes and utensils, full bath and shower, linens and towels, and picnic table and barbecue pit. Bring your own groceries, bath articles, paper goods, trash bags, river towels, charcoal, and matches. Two- or three-night minimum stay.

CIRCLE H LODGE

US 83
Leakey, TX 78873
361–882–9221
www.circlehranchtexas.com

Large, modern lodge accommodates up to eight people in a luxurious setting on an exotic animal ranch. The minimum stay for reservations made online is two nights. If you would like to stay for only a single night, please call to confirm availability before you arrive.

CYPRESS FRIO WATERS

273 Chalk Creek Rd.
Leakey, TX 78873
830–232–5955
www.cypressfrio.com

This family-owned ranch offers cabins on fifty acres with private access to the Frio River. Kitchenettes are furnished with stove, small refrigerator, microwave, coffee pot, dishes, silverware, glassware, pots and pans, dish soap, dish towels, and dish drainer. Sheets can be provided for $20.00 per stay. The cabins have air conditioning, ceiling fans, and walk-in showers. All cabins have a back porch that faces the river, which is about 75 yards away. Outside are picnic tables and fire rings as well as sport areas for volleyball, basketball, tetherball, horseshoes, ladder ball, soccer, football, and Frisbee. You can also rent tubes, kayaks, and canoes onsite.

FRIO PECAN FARM CABINS

144 RR 337
Leakey, TX 78873
830–232–78873
www.friopecanfarm.com

Vacation in a working pecan orchard! The property has eight vacation homes and seventeen log cabins for rent near the Ranch Road 337 crossing of the Frio River. The farm has won more than 550 awards for pecans in Texas and New Mexico. Eight different varieties of papershell pecans are grown. Pecans are harvested in October and November of each year but are available for sale year round. No smoking, no pets.

THE HISTORIC LEAKEY INN

527 US 83
Leakey, TX 787773
830–232–5246
www.leakeyinn.com

This historic inn from 1929 also has additional cabins. One-night stays are booked based upon occupancy, but usually there is a two-night minimum. Pet friendly. No smoking.

RIDING RIVER RANCH

RR 336
Leakey, TX 78873
361–215–5939
www.ridingriverranch.com

This property has several cabins with a private spring-fed lake and springs on a 3,400-acre ranch with river frontage. All cabins have central air and heat with Wi-Fi in most cabins. Satellite TV is available in every room. Kitchens are furnished with refrigerator, range, microwave, coffee pot, toaster, dishes, pots and pans, and utensils. All linens are provided (pillows, sheets, blankets, and towels). Picnic tables and barbecue pits. All you need is personal items and food. No pets, no smoking in cabins, no day use.

WHISKEY MOUNTAIN INN AND CABINS

US 83, 3.5 miles south of town
Leakey, TX 78873
830–232–4210
www.whiskeymountaininn.com

Stay in an old German home from 1869. During Prohibition, a whiskey distillery was developed in a cave in the mountain behind the property. The bootleggers were caught selling their product, and this area has been called "Whiskey Mountain" ever since. Several cabins are available, all with kitchens, baths, heat, and air. Pets under 25 pounds are welcome.

Normandy

US 277, 19 miles northwest of Eagle Pass
Population: 98

The community of Normandy owes its origin to the Lehmann Ranch, which was established at the site around 1878. In 1915 Lehmann Ranch was a military headquarters for US soldiers during the Mexican Revolution. In 1937 a post office opened with the name of Normandy.

Quemado

US 277, about 20 miles northwest of Eagle Pass
Population: 243

As you near the small community of Quemado, you leave the Lower Pecos Canyonlands. The landscape changes dramatically from the thorny desert scrub of the Chihuahuan Desert to lush pecan trees on both sides of US 277. Pecan orchards planted over forty years ago produce tons of delicious nuts in the alluvial soil just 1.5 miles east the Rio Grande. Look for signs for local sellers to buy the freshest, tastiest nuts for all your pies and cakes.

The Quemado Valley, for which the community is named, was designated the "burned valley" by Spanish explorers who believed the area had been parched by volcanic eruption. The first Catholic Mass on Texas soil is believed to have taken place in the valley in 1675.

In 1932 the Maverick County Irrigation Canal provided irrigation water. In 1936 Quemado had five grocery stores, three filling stations, a post office, a tourist camp, a community canning plant, a tile plant, a vegetable-loading platform, and a school.

Rocksprings is known as the Angora goat capital of the world. Photo by Thomas C. Self.

Rocksprings

US 377 and TX 55

Population: 1,285

Rocksprings, the county seat of Edwards County, is known as "the Angora goat capital of the world" and is located in the middle of sheep and goat country. Wool and mohair are still major economic drivers. Check out the bronze Angora goat sculpture on the corner near the courthouse.

History

The old spring located in the area drew travelers on the road that connected the US Army installations of Fort McKavett and Fort Clark. In 1877 Maj. John B. Jones's Texas Rangers assembled here to begin a major offensive to capture frontier outlaws. In addition to its military uses, the Fort Clark–Fort McKavett Road provided an accessible route for immigrants, cattle drovers, pioneer ranchers, mail carriers, and freighters. A town was founded in 1891 and soon had a post office. Tragedy stuck the town on April 12, 1927, when it was hit by an F5 tornado. The killer storm destroyed 235 buildings and killed 72 people and injured 205, almost one-third of the population at the time.

Things to Do

DEVIL'S SINKHOLE SOCIETY BAT TOUR

Stop at the Rocksprings Visitor Center on the square or call 830–683–2287 to make your reservations for an evening bat tour at Devil's Sinkhole State Natural Area. For more information, see the chapter on state parks.

Make reservations to see the bats at Devil's Sinkhole at the office in Rocksprings. Photo by Thomas C. Self.

Places to Visit

TEXAS MINIATURE MUSEUM

211 W. Main St.
Rocksprings, TX 78880
Hours: by appointment only

If you would like to visit the Texas Miniature Museum, please see the innkeeper at the Historic Rocksprings Hotel. The museum contains numerous dollhouses from different eras complete with furnishings.

Unique museums like this one in Rocksprings dot Southwest Texas. Photo by Thomas C. Self.

Groceries

LOWE'S SUPER S
102 TX 55
Rocksprings, TX 78880
830–683–2178

Restaurants

THE LOTUS THAI CAFE
100 W. Main St. (US 377)
Rocksprings, TX 78880
830–683–3711
Hours: Monday–Friday, 11:00 a.m.–2:30 p.m.

This small cafe is located across the street from the courthouse on the square. Come for the pad thai and stay for the spicy Bangkok Burger, Tom Yum soup, and crispy spring rolls. As authentic as you can get in this part of the world.

KINGBURGER DRIVE-IN
102 N. State St.
Rocksprings, TX 78880
830–683–4127
Hours: Daily, 10:00 a.m.–9:00 p.m.

Friendly, family-owned place serving burgers, enchiladas, and great onion rings.

Lodging

HISTORIC ROCKSPRINGS HOTEL
200 West Austin St.
Rocksprings, TX 78880
830–683–4212 or 713–515–2780
www.historicrockspringshotel.com

This venerable hotel opened its doors in the rough and ready days of 1916. Public rooms are tastefully decorated with antiques. Fourteen guest rooms offer king- and queen-size beds, and some have adjoining sitting rooms. Guests can enjoy the beautiful verandah, parlor, and library. One drawback is that no food is served at the hotel. Instead guests are invited to use the full kitchen in the building. Pots and pans, dishes, and other essentials are provided. Prices run from $85 to $95 per night. To visit the Texas Miniature Museum across the street, ask at the hotel reception desk.

The Historic Rocksprings Hotel offers comfortable, eclectic lodging. Photo by Thomas C. Self.

SORRELLS INN

205 E. Main St.
Rocksprings, TX 78880
830–683–1800
www.sorrellsinn.com

Clean rooms with Internet, TV, microwave, mini-fridge, and cold AC.

RED ROOSTER GUEST HOUSE AND THE HEN HOUSE

305 S. College St.
Rocksprings, TX 78880
830–683–5217 or 830–683–7156
www.redroosterguesthouse.com

The entire house sleeps six, with one queen-size bed, two singles, and a pull-out sofa. Full kitchen. Continental breakfast included. No pets, no smoking. Call the Hen House to make arrangements for a home-cooked meal when you arrive at the Red Rooster Guest House. They serve King Ranch chicken and other casseroles, soups, and desserts.

Utopia

RR 187 at junction with RR 1050

Population: 227

History

In 1856 an attempt was made to establish a communal living society modeled after the ideas of the French philosopher Charles Fourier near Sabinal Canyon. The attempt at communal living failed, but the hamlet was evermore called Utopia. Capt. William Ware, a soldier in the Texas Revolution, moved to the canyon with his son and six slaves in 1852. With 600 head of cattle and two ox-drawn wagons full of seeds, fruit trees, food, and tools, they had to move large boulders to get the wagons through the pass into the canyon. More settlers arrived in 1853, and by 1856 a combined store–post office had opened.

Day breaks in a small rural community of the Western Hill Country. Photo by Thomas C. Self.

In 1790 Spaniard Juan de Ugalde, commanding general for northern Mexico, united Comanches, Taovayas, and Tawakonis for a decisive victory over the Apaches at the Sabinal River Canyon. Indians continued to live in the area, however, and in 1839, John C. (Jack) Hays, legendary Texas Ranger, and Juan N. Seguín, former mayor of San Antonio and a captain in the Texas Revolution against Mexico, pursued a band of Comanches into Sabinal Canyon, where they destroyed newly deserted villages. Hays encountered the Comanches again two years later when eight Comanches were killed and two taken prisoner.

Conflicts with Comanches, Tonkawas, and other Native Americans in the area continued until 1876. By 1880 a stage was stopping weekly at the community, where 150 citizens supported two gristmills, a cotton gin, a blacksmith shop, a store, a school, and three churches.

Places to Visit

MAIN STREET UTOPIA

282 Main St.
Utopia, TX 78884
830–966–5544
www.mainstreetutopia.com
Hours: Tuesday–Saturday, 10:00 a.m.–4:00 p.m.

This French antique store is a surprising find in the Western Hill Country. The store imports country furniture and home accessories directly from France and also offers a variety of local products. Be sure to check out the winery supplies, books, and selection of women's clothing.

UTOPIA CITY PARK

240 Utopia Park Rd.
Utopia, TX 78884
Fee: $5.00

A nice swimming hole on the Sabinal River is located in this small city park.

SABINAL COUNTY MUSEUM

Main St. at Johnson St.
Utopia, TX 78884
830–966–3747
Hours: Saturday, 10:00 a.m.–4:00 p.m.; Sunday, 1:00 p.m.–4:00 p.m.
Admission: free

Learn about pioneer life through exhibits of farm implements, household items, Native American artifacts, and fossils and minerals from the Sabinal River Canyon. The museum also has an exhibit on World War II.

UTOPIA GOLF COURSE

20567 RR 187, 1 mile south of town
Utopia, TX 78884
830–966–5577
www.utopiagolf.com
Fee: $10.00–$20.00

Tee times are available but not required on this nine-hole course. A beautiful clubhouse serves beverages and offers a wide porch for lounging.

Groceries

UTOPIA GENERAL STORE

406 Main St.
Utopia, TX 78884
830–966–3444
Hours: Monday–Saturday, 6:00 a.m.–6:00 p.m.

Good selection of meat and produce plus general groceries.

Restaurants

LAUREL TREE RESTAURANT

18956 RR 187, 2.5 miles south of town
Utopia, TX 78884
830–966–5444
www.utopiagourmet.com
Hours: Saturdays only, 11:30 a.m.–1:00 p.m., 6:30 p.m.–8:00 p.m.
Pro-tip: Call early for reservations.

Chef Laurel Waters earned Le Grand Diplome in Cuisine, Pastry and Wine from Le Cordon Bleu in Paris. She went on to work at three of the finest restaurants in Provence. Now at her new restaurant she serves a five-course fixed-price lunch for $25.00 and dinner for $44.00. Menus change weekly, according to what is fresh and available locally. Sadly, Utopia is in a "dry" county, but diners are encouraged to bring their own wine to complement their meal. There is limited seating, so reservations are a must. Dressy casual attire.

LOST MAPLES CAFE

384 Main St. (RR 187)
Utopia, TX 78884
830–966–2221
www.lostmaplescafe.com
Hours: Sunday–Thursday, 7:00 a.m.–8:00 p.m.; Friday–Saturday, 7:00 a.m.–9:00 p.m.

Housed in a historic building from 1904, this restaurant is famous for homemade pies but also serves breakfast, salads, burgers, sandwiches, and Mexican food entrees. It also has a beautiful collection of vintage Formica tables and wooden booths from an old railroad dining car to enhance your experience.

Nostalgia is served up with the pancakes in Utopia. Photo by Thomas C. Self.

Lodging

SABINAL RIVER LODGE
RR 187 south
Utopia, TX 78884
830–966–3393
www.sabinalriverlodge.com

A fully furnished riverfront vacation rental lodge, brand new in June 2005. Satellite TV with DVD, Wi-Fi access, queen-size beds, Waverly linens, and fully stocked kitchenette with microwave oven, cooktop, and refrigerator. Two-night minimum during peak season. Call for possible one-night stays. Suite with two queen beds for $125.00 per night. No pets.

Uvalde

US 90
Population: 16,285

History

The town was originally founded as Encina in 1853, but raids by Tonkawa and Lipan Apaches discouraged permanent settlement for several years. When the county was organized in 1856, it took its name from Juan de Ugalde, a Mexican military leader who had been an Indian fighter in the area in the 1790s. The post office opened in 1857 under the name Uvalde. This was the wild frontier until the Galveston, Harrisburg and San Antonio Railway began operation in 1881. The city was incorporated in 1888. Several railroad lines expanded service during the next twenty years.

Uvalde is the birthplace of several notable characters. They include actors Dana Andrews and Matthew McConaughey, movie cowgirl Dale Evans, and the homegrown, Grammy Award–winning norteño band Los Palominos. Two prominent politicians also hail from Uvalde. John Nance "Cactus Jack" Garner (1868–1967) served two terms as vice-president under Franklin D. Roosevelt during the 1930s. Dolph Briscoe (1923–2010), a local rancher, was governor of Texas from 1973 to 1979.

Garner has been called the most powerful vice-president in US history. He served in the US House of Representatives more than twenty years and was

The Newton Boys

The Newton Boys were a criminal gang composed of brothers Willis, Joe, Jess, and Wylie ("Doc"), who operated mostly in Texas during the 1920s. They settled in Uvalde after their final release from prison. On December 31, 1914, Willis Newton robbed his first train near Uvalde of $4,700. While in prison, the brothers learned to use nitroglycerin to blow bank vaults and proceeded to use this technique several times after they were released.

Their last and most lucrative train robbery occurred in Rondout, Illinois, on June 12, 1924, when they held up a mail train. At $3 million, it was the largest train robbery in US history. They were sent to Leavenworth Prison, where Jess served nine months, Joe one year, Willis four years, and Doc six years, which included added time for an earlier escape attempt. They lived out their senior years back home in Uvalde. Willis lived to the age of ninety and wrote a book about their adventures. The money from their 1924 heist in Illinois was never found.

Arts and craft fairs are held often from spring through fall. Photo by the author.

speaker during the last two years of Herbert Hoover's presidency (1931–33). He was vice-president during President Franklin D. Roosevelt's first two terms (1933–1941). Garner was instrumental in passing much of the legislation for the New Deal that alleviated some of the worst suffering during the Great Depression. He also mentored Sam Rayburn and Lyndon B. Johnson from Texas and helped them in their political careers.

Garner was influential in the opening of Garner Army Air Field in Uvalde in 1941 for pilot training. When the facility was deactivated in June 1945, part of the airfield became the municipal airport. The more substantial buildings were renovated to become Southwest Texas Junior College.

Briscoe served in state government for over thirty years and championed reform during his two terms as governor, including the most extensive ethics and financial disclosure bill in state history. Under his administration, bills for open meetings and open records were passed as well as bills regulating lobbyists. He added more than $4 billion in new state funding for public schools and state universities and increased teacher salaries.

Today Uvalde is also home to an extensive automotive testing track (not open to the public). Continental Tires tests tire and vehicle performance on a variety of courses at the track.

Places to Visit

AVIATION MUSEUM AT GARNER FIELD

Uvalde Municipal Airport
201 Sul Ross Dr., Hangar 1
Uvalde, TX 78801
830–278–2552
Hours: Tuesdays and Fridays only, 9:00 a.m.–4:00 p.m.
Admission: donations accepted

This nonprofit museum is dedicated to preserving local and regional aviation history. The museum is housed in an original 1941 Garner Army Air Field hangar and has displays of aircraft and memorabilia from World War II. Vintage planes include a Liaison-4, a 1945 Piper L-4 Grasshopper, and a Burt Rutan Vari-Viggen.

BRISCOE ART AND ANTIQUE COLLECTION

200 East Nopal St.
Uvalde, TX 78801
830–278–6231
Hours: Monday–Friday, 9:00 a.m.–3:00 p.m.
Admission: free

Located in the lobby of the First State Bank is an unexpected treasure: works of art by such masters as Rembrandt, Gainsborough, Remington, Warren, Wood, and Salinas. The paintings were collected by Governor and Mrs. Dolph Briscoe.

BRISCOE-GARNER MUSEUM

333 North Park St.
Uvalde, TX 78001
830–278–5018
Hours: Tuesday–Saturday, 9:00 a.m.–4:00 p.m.
Admission: free

Housed in the home of John Nance Garner, the museum is one of four divisions of the Dolph Briscoe Center for American History, an organized research unit of The University of Texas at Austin. The Briscoe Center archives include the extensive John Nance Garner Scrapbook Collection, the only significant body of Garner papers that exists. Garner burned the majority of his papers upon his retirement as vice-president. The first floor contains an exhibit of his life.

This stately mansion houses the archives of Vice-President John Nance Garner. Photo by Thomas C. Self.

JANEY SLAUGHTER BRISCOE GRAND OPERA HOUSE

104 W. North St. on the square
Uvalde, TX 78801
830–278–4184

Hours: Sunday–Wednesday, 11:00 a.m.–8:00 p.m.; Thursday–Saturday, 11:00 a.m.–10:00 p.m.

Admission: Admission to the building is free, but fees are charged for concerts and programs.

This historic theater first opened in 1891 and remains the oldest functioning theater in Texas. Though the theater still hosts many events, the building is showing its age after being restored in 1982. The opera house now hosts community theater productions, children's theater, touring companies, and concerts. John Nance Garner bought the building in 1916, and his family later donated it to the city. The two-story Victorian building has arched windows, a copper roof, and a distinctive corner turret topped by a replica of a dragon weathervane. The original weathervane is displayed in the opera house's visitor center, along with historical photographs and artifacts from nearby Fort Inge.

The oldest theater in continuous use in Texas is located on the square in Uvalde. Photo by Thomas C. Self.

DALTON HOME

543 North Getty St.
Uvalde, TX 78801

This house was built in 1893 by Clara Horner. James T. Dalton, a former sea captain, bought the house in 1905. Private property; not open to the public.

KELLEY HOME

RR 187, about 5 miles south of Uvalde

Joe A. Kelley built this small two-room house in 1865. The house also has two shed rooms in the back. Private property; not open to the public.

NATIONAL FISH HATCHERY

754 City Rd. 203, off FM 481 (S. Old Eagle Pass Rd.)
Uvalde, TX 78801
830–278–2419

Hours: Monday–Friday, 7:00 a.m.–3:30 p.m., Saturday, 9:00 a.m.–3:30 p.m.; closed federal holidays

This is the top-producing warm-water federal hatchery in the nation, offering refuge to endangered fish species. Currently, the hatchery works with five threatened or endangered species and raises channel catfish for recreational fishing. Visitors are welcome and may participate in a guided or unguided tour. Facilities include fifty ponds, a newly completed intensive culturing facility, and a high-tech water supply system. The hatchery is also a good place for hiking, picnicking, and birding. The two-acre wildlife pond located across from the visitor center features a walking path with several points for bird-watching and wildlife observation. Yellow-headed blackbirds are seen here in some years, and breeders include Bullock's oriole and vermilion flycatcher. The hatchery is excellent for butterflies, and dragonflies are plentiful due to the emergent vegetation provided by the slough. This is a good site to see the blue grosbeak and the painted bunting, two of the area's summer nesting birds.

COOKS SLOUGH SANCTUARY AND NATURE PARK

CR 106 via US 83 south (S. Getty St.) and RR 117
Uvalde, TX 78801
830–278–4115
Hours: dawn to dusk
Admission: free

Cooks Slough is a man-made wetland birding habitat on the outskirts of Uvalde. The park includes 25 acres of wetland, two wildlife-viewing stations, and five shaded rest stations along the trails. There is also a 200-acre nature park that attracts wildlife. Although the park only has a couple of miles of hiking trails, the covered viewing pavilion provides an all-weather platform to see a variety of migratory and resident birds, dragonflies, and butterflies. It is also possible to spot deer, fox, and armadillos rooting around the brush. To get to Cooks Slough Preserve from US 90, head south on US 83, turn off onto FM 117, and make a right onto CR 106; the parking lot is at the end of the road.

Jim Bowie's Silver Mine

In the early 1700s the Spanish opened a silver mine somewhere near the present-day intersection of US 183 and RR 127 north of Uvalde. The ore was inferior, and the mine was abandoned; but fourteen shafts (some interconnecting) remain. Near the mine are remnants of a fortification made by thirty men under the leadership of James Bowie, later a hero of the siege of the Alamo in 1836. In 1831, while at work at this mine, Bowie's men repulsed a Comanche attack in a fierce, all-day battle. The hero of the fight was Bowie's slave, "Black Jim Bowie," who risked his life by leaving the fortification to bring water to the besieged.

Groceries

There are several large supermarkets in Uvalde, some with pharmacies and bakeries. There are also several stand-alone pharmacies and many gas stations. If you are going north to the riverside resorts, this is the place to buy supplies.

H-E-B SUPERMARKET AND PHARMACY

201 E. Main St.
Uvalde, TX 78801
830–278–3352
Hours: Daily, 6:00 a.m.–11:00 p.m.; pharmacy, 9:00 a.m.–9:00 p.m. (may vary).

Get all your food supplies for enjoying the rivers, whether you'll be in a cabin, RV, or tent. The store may also have water toys and inflatable tubes during summer.

WALMART SUPERCENTER AND PHARMACY

3100 E. Main St.
Uvalde, TX
830–278–9117
Hours: Daily, 24 hours

In addition to a large grocery section, this is the place to pick up camping gear, automotive supplies, clothing, or a big-screen TV. The store will also have inflatable tubes for floating on the river in the summer.

Restaurants

LIVE OAK DRIVE THRU

128 S. High St.
Uvalde, TX 78801
830–278–3998
Hours: Monday–Saturday, 10:00 a.m.–4:00 p.m.

This place doesn't look like much, but don't let that fool you. Mexican favorites like tortilla soup and gorditas are made to order. Fillings include carne guisada, picadillo, and nopalitos. Chicken fajitas and brisket plates are also served. This is one of those "secret" hometown places that has been featured in *Southern Living* magazine and on the Food Channel. I recommend the brisket gordita with its savory filling and crispy, light shell. Cash only.

EL HERRADERO DE JALISCO

224 W. Main St.
1408 N. Getty St.
Uvalde, TX 78801
830–278–3600
Hours: Daily, 6:30 a.m.–10:00 p.m.

This family-owned Mexican food restaurant has two locations serving carne asada, enchiladas, puffy tacos, menudo, burritos, and gorditas as well as children's plates and breakfast. Full bar.

SUNRISE CAFE

510 W. Main St.
Uvalde, TX 78801
830–278–6100
Hours: Daily, 6:00 a.m.–2:00 p.m.

Good breakfast place. Also has a soup and salad bar and serves fried chicken breast for about $8.00. Fried fish, chopped steak and mashed potatoes, green beans, and chocolate cake are also available.

JACK'S STEAK HOUSE

2500 E. Main St.
Uvalde, TX 78801
830–278–9955
Hours: Monday–Saturday, 11:00 a.m.–10:00 p.m.

Look for the log cabin along Main Street and pull on in! Jack's serves traditional steaks and sides such as fried okra and mac and cheese. The sourdough bread is delicious. Service can be spotty, however. Full bar.

THE TEA ROOM

103 N. West St., on the square
Uvalde, TX 78801
830–486–0722
Hours: Monday–Friday, 11:00 a.m.–2:00 p.m.

Try the roasted poblano soup! Sandwiches and daily specials such as buffalo chicken salad will keep you happy.

THE GOURMET COFFEE CUP

2001 E. Main St.
Uvalde, TX 78801
830–275–3539
Hours: Monday–Saturday, 7:00 a.m.–2:00 p.m.

This cozy spot makes a great pumpkin latte, mocha frappe, and other specialty coffees. Belgian waffles, southwestern omelets, chicken chipotle wraps, broccoli cheese soup, and organic smoothies are also on the menu.

TOWN HOUSE RESTAURANT

2105 E. Main St.
Uvalde, TX 78801
830–278–2428
Hours: Daily, 6:00 a.m.–10:00 p.m.

This traditional American-style place has a good breakfast, a lunch buffet, and nightly dinner specials. The Sunday buffet usually includes turkey and dressing, chicken-fried steak, and baked chicken for about $12.00.

NAPOLI'S

2217 E. Main St.
Uvalde, TX 78801
830–278–2210
Hours: Daily, 11:00 a.m.–10:00 p.m.

You'll find a wide variety of homemade Italian food here. Try the veal marsala, chicken piccata, or seafood Napoli. The sausage and cheese calzones are huge, and don't forget the cannolis for dessert!

Fascinating antique shops are often found in small towns. Photo by author.

Lodging

Pro-tip: If you are traveling through and just need to stay one night, Uvalde is your best bet until Del Rio. Most lodging in the Western Hill Country north of Uvalde consists of resort rentals for a week or more.

HAMPTON INN

2714 E. Main St.
Uvalde, TX 77801
830–278–1300

Free hot breakfast, free business center, fitness room, Wi-Fi, 75 units, 24/7 free coffee, complimentary cookies (5:00 p.m.–7:00 p.m.).

AMERICAS BEST VALUE INN

701 E. Main St.
Uvalde, TX 77801
830–278–5671

Playground, pool, unpretentious standard motel with 87 units.

HOLIDAY INN EXPRESS

2801 E. Main St.
Uvalde, TX 78801
830–278–7300

Fitness center, outdoor pool and hot tub, Wi-Fi, free hot breakfast, cinnamon rolls, refrigerators, microwaves, coffee makers, laundry room; 80 units.

HONEYSUCKLE COTTAGE AND BEE HOUSE

115 Puccini Lane
Uvalde, TX 78801
830–278–3018
www.honeysucklestation.com

Honeysuckle Cottage is a two-bedroom, fully furnished cottage with linens, covered patio, fenced backyard, VCR, and DVD player. Bee House, a one-bedroom, fully furnished guesthouse with linens, is located behind Honeysuckle Cottage and just across from Uvalde Memorial Hospital.

INN OF UVALDE

810 East Main St.
Uvalde, TX 78801
830–278–9173

Pool, restaurant, complimentary breakfast, refrigerators, and microwaves; 71 units. Pet friendly.

QUALITY INN

920 East Main St.
Uvalde, TX 78801
830–278–4511

Pool, restaurant, 114 units. Pet friendly.

LIVE OAKS BED AND BREAKFAST

6 Tanglewood
Uvalde, TX 78801
830–591–2340
www.liveoaksbnb.com

Four large, distinctly decorated rooms in a large modern home; queen-size beds. Pool and oak-covered backyard. Great breakfast.

Country roads beg to be explored in Southwest Texas. Photo by Thomas C. Self.

MOTEL 6

924 E. Main St.
Uvalde, TX 78801
830–900–7084

This budget motel has 37 units with kitchenettes; pet friendly.

CHALK BLUFF PARK

1108 Chalk Bluff Rd., off TX 15
Uvalde, TX 78801
830–278–5515
www.chalkbluffriverresort.com

Located about 1 mile off TX 55 north of Uvalde, right on the Nueces River, Chalk Bluff Park has everything: cabins, tent and RV sites, pony rides, tubing and kayaking, putt-putt golf, fishing, and hunting packages.

Robinson Massacre

A legendary Indian battle took place near Chalk Bluff in 1861 when two well-known Indian fighters were ambushed by a band of twenty hostile Indians. The tall, red-haired Henry Robinson inspired roaming Comanches or Kiowas to paint his picture on a rock near the Llano River. Robinson and his companion, Henry Adams, were en route to Camp Wood when they were attacked with blood-chilling screams. The Indians killed the two men, then took both their scalps—and Robinson's beard, too. Robinson's family fought them off, however, when they attacked the homestead. Since then, the area has been much quieter.

Vanderpool

RR 337 and RR 187

Population: 20

History

Formerly known as Bugscuffle, Vanderpool is about a 1.5-hour drive north of Uvalde. The Sabinal Valley, in which Vanderpool is located, was first settled in the 1850s. Jose Texaso received this land from the Republic of Texas in 1849. Settlement was temporarily abandoned in the late 1860s due to raiding by Comanche Indians. Comanches, Apaches, Tonkawas, and Kickapoos lived in the area, and Apaches are known to have established villages in the vicinity. A post office was established in 1886, closed in 1889, and then reopened in 1902. The town was named for the first postmaster, L. B. Vanderpool. A school, known as Bugscuffle School, operated for one year in 1887–88. The Oxford English Dictionary provides no definition for "bugscuffle," but some say it means "a small disagreement or fight."

Places to Visit

LONE STAR MOTORCYCLE MUSEUM

36517 RR 187, 4 miles north of town
Vanderpool, TX 78885
830–966–6103
www.lonestarmotorcyclemuseum.com
Hours: Friday–Sunday, 10:00 a.m.–5:00 p.m., March through November
Admission: $6.00

Come see over 50 classic motorcycles from 1910 on. The museum has a great big sign, so you can't miss it.

Groceries

LOST MAPLES GENERAL STORE

33533 RR 187
Vanderpool, TX 78885
830–966–3568

Great little country store with gas and diesel.

Restaurants

ACE CAFE

36517 RR 187
Vanderpool, TX 78885
830–966–6103
www.lonestarmotorcyclemuseum.com
Hours: Friday–Sunday, 10:00 a.m.–5:00 p.m., March through November

Located inside Lone Star Motorcycle Museum, the cafe serves hamburgers, Aussie meat pies, and salads.

Lodging

Once you leave Uvalde, drop-in one-night motel accommodations are hard to find in the Western Hill Country. Most resort cabins rent for several nights at a time and are reserved early. Tent and RV camping is also very popular, and reservations are recommended. Also see the websites listed in chapter 1.

FOXFIRE CABINS

117 Olsen Ranch Rd., off RR 187, 4 miles north of town
Vanderpool, TX 78885
830–966–2200
www.foxfirecabins.com

Located on the banks of the Sabinal River, these seven fully furnished, two-bedroom, one-bath cabins sleep from four to sixteen; many other vacation homes are also available. Rates vary from $120.00 to $240.00 per night. Some cabins accept pets, but inquire first. No smoking, no tents. Guest laundry. No meals are served, so bring your own food.

THE LODGES OF LOST MAPLES

77 Lower Sabinal River Rd. at junction with RR 337, 4 miles west of town
Vanderpool, TX 78888
830–966–5178
www.lostmaplescabins.com

Five fully furnished cabins, each with fireplace, kitchenette, central air and heat, and bathroom. No pets, no smoking. Call for reservations and rates.

Red maple leaves glow in the late fall around Lost Maples State Natural Area. Photo by Thomas C. Self.

A PEACE OF HEAVEN

1856 Evans Creek Rd.
Vanderpool, TX 78885
830–966–5198
www.apeaceofheaven.org

This property has three fully equipped, antique-filled log cabins that sleep up to seven persons each. There are two separate bedrooms plus a daybed in the living room. Full kitchens are equipped with a stove, coffee maker with gourmet coffee, microwave, and refrigerator. All dishes, cooking utensils, linens, and towels are supplied. Family-owned and -operated on twenty-five acres. Cabins are $125.00 per night. Three RV spots go for $20.00 to $25.00. No smoking. Pets allowed on leash.

FARHAVEN FARM

Off RR 187 between Vanderpool and Utopia
Vanderpool, TX 78885
830–966–3723
www.farhavenfarm.com

This horse-friendly farm of seventy-six acres is in Sabinal Canyon between Lost Maples State Park and the town of Utopia. You can bring your horse and enjoy the county! Cabins have fully equipped kitchens, coffee and tea, towels, linens, barbecue grills, fire pits, firewood, and a movie and CD library. Laundry service is available. A barn for horses has four twelve-by-twelve-foot stalls with rubber mats and shavings; a half-acre shaded paddock is enclosed with five-foot woven-wire horse fence ($20 per night per horse). Feed and hay available locally. Pet friendly if reserved ahead of time. No smoking. No horses for hire.

Longhorns graze peacefully in a typical Texas scene. Photo by Thomas C. Self..

8

Ghost Towns

Abandoned buildings with doors banging in the wind, tumbleweeds blowing across the road, a big sky overhead, and a feeling of desolation that comes from the remains of what once was a bustling place—that's a ghost town. Southwest Texas has more than its share of such places, all of which are interesting to visit. Well, all except one, because it's underwater!

This building on the edge of Langtry shows the ravages of weather and time. Photo by Thomas C. Self.

Carta Valley

US 377, about 38 miles northeast of Del Rio

Population: 12

Pro-tip: No gas or other facilities are available. Do not trespass on private property.

Settlers arrived in the area of Carta Valley in 1898. By 1906 there was a general store and a post office. The settlement briefly had a population of about 150 in 1960s. In 1978 the community had a school, a church, and a few dwellings, some of which remain.

Devils River

Under Lake Amistad

The town of Devils River was located near the mouth of the Devils River and the Rio Grande prior to the building of Amistad Dan in 1968. Founded as a station on the Galveston, Harrisburg and San Antonio Railway in 1882, Devils River once had a population of fifty to sixty people. In the 1940s about twenty families lived there. When the Amistad Dam and Reservoir were built in 1968, the entire town was flooded and is now under water.

Three hydroelectric dams were constructed on the Devils River in the 1920s by Central Power and Light Company. To encourage the use of electricity, the company also sold stoves and vacuums and gave classes on cooking and cleaning with electric appliances. The three Devils River electrical generating plants were in use until 1965, when the Amistad Dam was completed. Although Amistad Dam is more technologically advanced, it produces only a fraction of the energy that the original three CP&L dams were able to produce. Today the remains of the three old plants lie under Amistad Reservoir without even a historical marker.

Dolores

US 90, 7 miles west of Brackettville

During the time when Texas was part of Mexico, John Charles Beales brought fifty-nine settlers to a spot here on Las Moras Creek in 1833 to start a colony on the frontier. Mexico had granted Beales more than 50,000,000 acres in what is today western Texas and eastern New Mexico, plus much of the Rio Grande Valley. The small settlement was named for his wife, but it was short-lived, as Indian raids and drought soon took their toll. Beales's Rio Grande colony disappeared during the Texas Revolution against Mexico.

Juno

RR 163, 40 miles north of Comstock

Population: 2

Pro-tip: Beware of hunters, especially in winter, and ranchers with rifles. Do not trespass on private property. No gas or other facilities are available. If there is more than a few inches of water at any low-water crossing on the Devils River, please play it safe. Turn around, don't drown.

The community of Juno was established sometime in the early 1880s. By 1900 it was a ranching center with a general store, a hotel, and two schools. Local legend says the name of the town came from the daily menu offerings of beans and beer in the only cafe. When asked what was for lunch, everyone just said, "ju know."

After a peak population of 80, in 1964 the number of Juno's residents began to decline. The post office closed in 1975, and the last reported business closed in 1984.

The wind blows through the few old buildings left at Juno. Photo by author.

Laguna

TX 55 and FM 334, about 16 miles northwest of Uvalde

Population: no official data

Laguna was a center for shipping wool, hides, and livestock in the 1880s. The community was called Norwood when a post office opened in 1879, and Good Luck before that. By 1890 the town had a general store, gristmill, cotton gin, and a pecan dealership, but by 1988 the village was abandoned.

Langtry

Off US 90, about 60 miles west of Del Rio

Population: 14

Pro-tip: Do not trespass on private property, which is virtually everything you see in the Lower Pecos Canyonlands. Ranchers are serious about this and do carry firearms. A telephoto lens will save you a lot of grief.

Some people may complain that Langtry, with its fluctuating population of around fourteen, is not really a ghost town. But take a look around and you will find abandoned adobe ruins, empty stores, and long vistas. Langtry, originally called Eagle Nest, was created in 1882 as a water stop for steam locomotives. The town was most likely named for George Langtry, who led the railroad building crew. Lore, though, links the town's most famous inhabitant to its naming; Roy Bean, who owned a local saloon and served as justice of the peace, became known as the Law West of the Pecos. He was enamored of Lillie Langtry, a popular British actress, and although she was probably not the town's namesake, she did visit here in the early twentieth century.

Places to Visit

JUDGE ROY BEAN VISITOR CENTER AND BOTANICAL GARDEN

Loop 25, off US 90
Langtry, TX 78871
432–291–3340

Hours: Daily, 8:00 a.m.–5:00 p.m.

Admission: free

Pro-tip: Cold water and air-conditioning available here! Wheelchair accessible.

One of the best-kept secrets in Southwest Texas is the Judge Roy Bean Visitor Center and Botanical Garden, run by the Texas Department of Transportation. In addition to free Texas highway maps and tourist information,

Judge Roy Bean named his saloon after the beautiful Lillie Langtry, mistress to England's Edward VII. At the time this was like naming a saloon after Marilyn Monroe. Photo by Thomas C. Self.

this wonderful little spot is home to the original historic buildings built by Judge Roy Bean in the 1880s as well as a fabulous botanical garden featuring over 100 varieties of plants of the Chihuahuan Desert.

The center preserves the Jersey Lilly saloon and home where the colorful Judge Roy Bean dispensed "Law West of the Pecos" in the 1880s. The saloon has the original bar and a big poolroom, which was also sometimes used as a courtroom. The Langtry Opera House was actually the home where Bean lived. Note the thick adobe walls and cool breezeway.

Bean came to the work camp of Vinegarroon several miles east of here in 1882 to sell whiskey to the Chinese and other railroad construction workers. When the temporary camp disbanded, Bean came here as justice of the peace. Langtry did not have a jail, so all cases were settled by fines, which Bean pocketed entirely. Bean is known to have sentenced only two men to hang, one of whom escaped. Although only district courts were legally allowed to grant divorces, Bean did so anyway, pocketing $10.00 per divorce. He charged $5.00 for a wedding but didn't offer new couples much hope. He ended all wedding ceremonies with "May God have mercy on your souls." Several movies and at least one TV show have been made about Bean's life.

Hundreds of wild plants from the Chihuahuan Desert were collected to form the botanical garden at Langtry. Photo by Thomas C. Self.

The botanical garden introduces visitors to the plants of the Chihuahuan Desert. Most of the plants were gathered from the wild on surrounding land when the visitor center opened in 1970. Each plant is labeled with its name and uses. Many native desert plants have medicinal uses, and most were used by ancient people in many ways. This is a great place to spend an hour or so learning about the Chihuahuan Desert with a little history to boot! Be sure to bring your camera. Absolutely worth a stop.

VASHTI SKILES COMMUNITY CENTER

Torres Ave.
Langtry, TX 78871

From the Judge Roy Bean Visitor Center, drive south down Torres Avenue and turn left to the large white wooden building with the metal roof. The Vashti Skiles Community Center was the school, back when Langtry had more population. The small house to the northeast was the teacherage, or house where the teacher lived. It was not uncommon around the turn of the twentieth century for rural schools to include living accommodations as part of a teacher's pay. Typically, both schools and teacherages were built by neighbors on land donated by a member of the community. Today the school building is used for community meetings of all sorts. Not open to the public.

TORRES HOME

Torres Ave.
Langtry, TX 78871

Cesario Torres donated land from his ranch to build a depot and water stop at Langtry for the new train in 1883. His son Juan Pablo Torres served alternately with Roy Bean as justice of the peace for the village. Today the ruins of his home are all that remain.

Adobe ruins haunt the ghost town of Langtry. Photo by Thomas C. Self.

DODD STORE

Torres Ave.
Langtry, TX 78871

This wooden structure is now completely collapsed, but in 1894 it was a bustling general store owned by William H. Dodd. He and his wife also owned a boardinghouse and were active in the young community. During the Mexican Revolution (1910–20), Dodd reportedly supplied arms and other goods to the revolutionaries. Later he served as justice of the peace in Langtry.

CANYON VIEWS

Drive to the south end of Torres Avenue and admire the gorgeous view of the canyon along the Rio Grande. The cliffs to the south are in Mexico, so this is about as close as you can get without a passport. Notice the twin caves downstream on the US side of the river. The side canyon opening onto the Rio Grande towards the east is Eagle Nest Canyon.

The southernmost buffalo jump in North America is down Eagle Nest Canyon. Thousands of years ago huge herds of buffalo and other animals jumped to their death off the rim. Archaeologists have found bones from over 800 animals at the base of the cliff in a place known as Bonfire Shelter. Deep inside the shelter, archaeologists even found bones from saber-toothed tigers that lived about 12,000 years ago during the last Ice Age. Do not attempt to enter the canyon. The canyon is on private property, and the owner does not take kindly to trespassers.

WAGON WHEEL CAFE AND STORE

US 90, just west of Langtry
432–291–3227
Emergency food, beer, and gas are available during business hours. If no one is there, the place is not open. A gallon of gas cost $4.50 at the time of this writing, when it was selling everywhere else for about $2.00 per gallon. There is a basic motel with about four rooms next to the cafe and hookups for six RVs in town.

Montell

TX 55, about 30 miles north of Uvalde
Population: no official data

Montell is located in a canyon just north of where Montell Creek joins the Nueces River. In 1762 the Spanish sent Father Diego Jiménez and ten soldiers to found Mission Nuestra Señora de la Candelaria del Cañón on the west bank of the Nueces River near this site in hopes of converting the Lipan Apaches to Christianity. The Apaches apparently found no appeal in the mission except as a refuge from the Comanches, and by 1771 the mission had been abandoned.

The town itself was named for Charles S. DeMontel, a Prussian immigrant who served in the Confederate Army and surveyed the Nueces Canyon. He established a camp near the present townsite. John R. Baylor, Indian fighter and self-proclaimed Confederate governor of Arizona Territory during the Civil War, moved into the area in 1878. He recruited others to settle the town with the intention of forming a Christian community. He was the nephew of Judge R.E.B. Baylor, for whom Baylor University is named. A post office opened in Montell in 1879, and two churches were established around 1890. The Episcopal Church of the Ascension, which still holds services, is known for its stained glass window, donated by the estate of John Jacob Astor. The post office closed after 1930, and the population declined. Look for historical markers on the east side of Texas 55 near the intersection with County Road 415.

Cactus blooms can be brilliant purple, red, pink, or yellow. Photo by Thomas C. Self.

Pumpville

RR 1865, west of Langtry and about 2 miles north of US 90

Population: about 20

Pro-tip: No gas or other facilities are available. Do not trespass on private property.

Like several other communities in the Lower Pecos Canyonlands, Pumpville started as a water stop for the railroad. In the early 1880s steam trains had to take on water and fuel quite frequently. Railroad workers and a few ranching families soon built a small village to serve this purpose. Several businesses and churches soon appeared. The only building still in use today is the Pumpville Baptist Church, which holds occasional services.

A famous train robbery occurred here in 1889. Three armed robbers stopped a westbound passenger train near Pumpville. One was killed during the skirmish, and the other two were later caught by Texas Rangers. One went to prison, and the other died shortly afterward of tuberculosis.

Baxter's Curve Train Robbery, March 13, 1912

When a westbound train stopped to take on water between Dryden and Sanderson just about midnight, it was attacked by the Hole in the Wall Gang, also known as the Wild Bunch. Members of the gang included Ben Kilpatrick, known as the Tall Texan because he was tall and good-looking; Robert L. Parker, also known as Butch Cassidy; Henry Longabaugh, known as the Sundance Kid; and Ole Hobek.

The gang captured the train and the crew and proceeded to rob the mail car and the safe. As they were walking through one of the freight cars, David Trousdale, the express manager for Wells Fargo assigned to the train, picked up an ice maul that was sitting on top of a crate of oysters. When he got a moment of opportunity, Trousdale hit Hobek with the maul and bashed his brains out. Then he shot Kilpatrick.

The robbers were armed not only with guns, but also with six sticks of dynamite, a box of dynamite caps, and a pint of nitroglycerin.

For his bravery, Trousdale was awarded $1,000.00 by Wells Fargo, another $1,000.00 by the federal government, $500.00 from the Southwestern Pacific Railroad, and a gold watch. Passengers on the train took up a collection for Trousdale of $51.00 on the stop and also contributed a gold watch fob set with a diamond to demonstrate their appreciation of his efforts.

Hobek and Kilpatrick are buried in Sanderson, but Butch Cassidy and the Sundance Kid got away. At least that's one theory. Several other accounts claim that Butch and Sundance were in South America at the time of this train robbery.

What really happened to Butch Cassidy and the Sundance Kid is unclear. A man named William Phillips who died in 1937 claimed he was the real Butch Cassidy. The truth may never be known. What is known is that Butch and Sundance robbed millions of dollars from various banks and trains during their career in crime.

The two characters were immortalized in the 1969 movie *Butch Cassidy and the Sundance Kid*, starring Paul Newman and Robert Redford.

Shumla

US 90, about 15 miles west of Comstock

Pro-tip: Slow down! You'll miss it!

Shumla began as a construction camp for the railroad in 1882. The place was named by a railroad engineer who thought the area looked like the countryside around the Ottoman fortress of Shumla in the Balkans. Once regular east-west rail traffic began, Shumla became a section point with a depot, water tank, and foreman's house. A post office was established in 1906 but was only open until 1909. A freight station continued to function at the site into the 1930s, but it was reduced to a flag stop by 1973. By the 1980s all that remained were the ruins of an old store, service station, and 1930s-era motel along the highway.

The abandoned ruins of Shumla sit silently along the highway. Photo by Jack Johnson.

9

Scenic Routes

Taking the back roads can almost always lead to something special. Even US 90, the southern route from San Antonio to Big Bend, can show you something spectacular if you know where to look and slow down just a little bit to enjoy the country. This chapter features ten scenic drives that take you to remote areas and lucky surprises in Southwest Texas.

The Twisted Sisters Trail

RR 337, 336, and 335; start and finish in Leakey, a loop of about 78 miles

One of the favorite routes for motorcycle riders follows the canyons and steep hills in the Western Hill Country on Ranch Roads 337, 336, and

Tight curves and great scenery thrill riders on the Twisted Sisters route. Photo by Thomas C. Self.

335. Called "The Twisted Sisters," this route in not for the timid. There are many tight, twisty curves with shear dropoffs and not much in the way of guardrails in many places. Drivers are urged to slow down and use caution. Hard-core cyclists sometimes train on this route, too, so watch out for them. If you are new to motorcycle riding, then this is not the ride for you. If you like scenic panoramic views, however, bring your camera, take this ride, and hold on!

Gas up at Leakey (where there is also a very good motorcycle shop), then go north on US 83 for just about a mile and look for Ranch Road 336 on the left. Hold left onto Ranch Road 336 and continue north until you meet Texas 41. Turn left onto Texas 41. Go west for 15 miles or so until you see Ranch Road 335 on the left. Go south on Ranch Road 335 to Camp Wood, then take a left onto Ranch Road 337 to finish out the loop when you hit Leakey again.

This route has few gas stations and many twists and turns over large hills. This roller coaster is not heavily traveled, but beware, as sharp turns have taken many motorcyclists down. And although the surface is mostly in very good condition, always watch for loose gravel, deer, and slow-moving trucks or, even worse, tourists. Fun drive.

Idyllic country drives abound in Southwest Texas. Photo by Thomas C. Self.

The Bullhead Canyon Trail

RR 335 and CR 2631, start and finish in Barksdale, a loop of about 10 miles

Start in Barksdale and head north on Ranch Road 335. Turn right onto County Road 2631, which travels along Bullhead Creek. If you're lucky, you'll see giraffes loping across the meadows. You will crisscross Bullhead Creek several times as you continue along the road. Go past a very interesting white wall, going rather slowly until the paved road becomes a dirt path through the trees. At that point you must turn around and head back. A beautiful excursion.

The Buffalo Soldiers and Black Seminole Indian Scouts Trail

RR 481, US 57, US 277, TX 131, RR 3348, US 90, Uvalde to Pecos River High Bridge, about 200 miles

To follow the lives of the Buffalo Soldiers and their brethren, the Black Seminole Indian scouts, start in Uvalde at Fort Inge (off Ranch Road 140), where Buffalo Soldiers were stationed after the Civil War. Then take Ranch Road 481 south to US 57 south to Fort Duncan in Eagle Pass. Black Seminole Indian scouts were attached to this unit in 1870. From Eagle Pass, take US 277 west to Normandy, then Texas 131 north to Brackettville and Fort Clark, where both groups were stationed from 1870 to 1914. Stop by the Black Seminole Scout Cemetery on Ranch Road 3348 to pay your respects to four Medal of Honor winners among the Black Seminole scouts. From Fort Clark go west on US 90 to Del Rio, then continue to the Pecos River High Bridge, to view the battle site near the mouth of the Pecos River that resulted in three Medals of Honor for these men.

The New Money and Old Art Trail

RR 481 and US 57, Uvalde to Galloway White Shaman Preserve (west of Del Rio), about 165 miles

On a Friday, go to the First State Bank at 200 W. Nopal Street in Uvalde, where the bankers keep the money, to see paintings by Rembrandt, Gainsborough, and others collected by former Texas first lady Janey Briscoe. When you have examined these works to your content, take Ranch Road 481 and continue south on US 57 to the Kickapoo Lucky Eagle Casino in Eagle

Pass. Why? To win yourself some money of your own to put in the bank, of course! Or maybe to buy a piece of art from a local artist.

You can easily spend the night in Eagle Pass or continue northwest on Texas 277 to Del Rio (55 miles). You can spend the night in Del Rio if you wish or proceed out US 90 west 41 miles to Seminole Canyon State Park and Historic Site, where there is camping. On Saturday morning take the 10:00 a.m. tour of Fate Bell Shelter at the park to see rock art several thousands of years old, then continue to the Galloway White Shaman Preserve without delay to join the tour at 12:30 p.m. Try to arrive at the gate on the north side of US 90 just 1.5 miles west of the state park by noon to have enough time. Compare the different techniques and purposes of the art you see on this trip. Then think about the value of the art and the money it takes to preserve it. That might make you want to go back to the casino!

The Bat Trail

Kickapoo Cavern State Park to Rocksprings to Concan, about 126 miles total

To see the show at all three bat caves in the area, visitors will need three evenings, because that's when the bats fly out for their nightly feeding frenzy. Make reservations for tours and lodging before starting out. Camping is

Bats at Kickapoo Cavern fly out in the early evening to the delight of visitors. Courtesy Texas Parks and Wildlife Department.

available at Kickapoo Cavern State Park and Garner State Park, with hotels found in Rocksprings or Concan. Register for the Devil's Sinkhole tour at the Devil's Sinkhole Visitor Center in Rocksprings. See the chapter on state parks for more information.

The Aviation History Trail

TX 55 and US 90, Camp Wood to Del Rio, about 79 miles

Start at Camp Wood, where Charles Lindberg made a surprise landing on Main Street in 1924. He clipped a post and crashed into a building. Not his finest hour, but typical of the early days of aviation. Next take Texas 55 south to Uvalde to the Aviation Museum at the Uvalde airport to see the exhibits. From there take US 90 west to Del Rio to drive by Laughlin Air Force Base and see the Laughlin Heritage Foundation Museum. Be sure to see the

The *Vin Fiz*

The first airplane in Val Verde County arrived on October 26, 1911. It was piloted by Cal Rodgers, a daredevil attempting the first transcontinental air flight in a Wright Brothers plane called the *Vin Fiz*. He left from Sheepshead Bay, New York, on September 17, 1911, and finally arrived in Pasadena, California, on November 5, 1911. In the meantime, he crashed fifteen times and required numerous repairs. A supply train followed him the entire way with spare parts.

The Armour food company sponsored the trip and named the plane after a new grape soda that the company was introducing. Rodgers was trying to win a $50,000.00 prize being offered by William Randolph Hearst but missed the deadline by nineteen days.

Rodgers flew from Sabinal to Del Rio, where he stopped briefly for lunch. The rough country west of Del Rio worried him because of the steep canyons and desert. He flew with the Rio Grande on his left and the Southwestern Pacific railroad tracks on his right, crisscrossing into Mexico several times. He was spotted in Langtry, stopped briefly in Dryden for oil, and landed in Sanderson for the night.

Rodgers took several hours of flying lessons from the Wright Brothers before he bought their Model B pusher bi-plane, also known as the EX. The plane flew about 50 mph and cruised at about 3,000 feet. The plane could not cross the Rocky Mountains, so Rodgers chose a southwestern route for his flight. Rodgers died in a plane crash in 1912, only five months after his record-setting flight. The *Vin Fiz* is now in the Smithsonian Air and Space Museum.

exhibit on the Cuban missile crisis of 1962. Have lunch in Del Rio like aviation pioneer Cal Rodgers. In 1911 he landed his plane, *Vin Fiz*, in Del Rio for lunch on his first transcontinental flight. Residents in Langtry, farther out west on US 90, waved to him overhead later that day as he followed the Rio Grande west.

The Great Train Robbery Trail

US 90, Uvalde to Sanderson, about 189 miles

Start in Uvalde, where the Newton Gang robbed their first train in 1914 and lived out their golden years. Then take US 90 past Del Rio to the Pecos River High Bridge and stop at the overlook on the south side of the highway. Look to the northwest of the Pecos River toward the location of the Silver Spike, commemorating the completion of the southern route of the transcontinental railroad in 1883. Continue on US 90 west to Comstock, the site of the Cow Creek robbery in 1896. To get a real feel for the isolation of the area and understand how easy it might have been to pull off these heists, continue on US 90 west past Langtry, then turn right onto Ranch Road 1865 to see the site of the train robbery at Pumpville in 1889. Backtrack to US 90 and continue west to Dryden and Sanderson to see the desolate land where

Justice could be swift a hundred years ago in rural Texas. Photo by Thomas C. Self.

the Hole in the Wall Gang robbed a train in 1912. Before or after this trip, watch the 1969 movie *Butch Cassidy and the Sundance Kid*, starring Paul Newman and Robert Redford, and *The Newton Boys*, released in 1998, starring Matthew McConaughey.

The Pecos Crossing Trail

RR 1024, Comstock to Pandale, about 59 miles

At Comstock, fill up with gas and other essentials because none are available on this route. Take Ranch Road 1024 just west of Comstock for 53 miles to Pandale. Continue on for 5.5 miles on a dirt road to the river crossing. Follow the signs to Pandale Crossing. The Pecos River is broad and shallow at this crossing, making it a perfect place to get in the water! Visitors can enjoy fishing, swimming, floating, kayaking, wildlife viewing, and birdwatching.

When you reach the Pandale Crossing Resort, take the dirt road to the right and go over the bridge. The Amistad National Recreation Area maintains a gravel access road to the river immediately on the left of the bridge. Park on the large limestone slab by the water. There is no shade or facilities of any kind. Bring your own lunch and pack out your trash. Pandale Crossing Resort rents basic cabins with bath, shower, kitchenette, and AC.

The Pecos River spreads out near Pandale for easy kayaking. Photo by Jack Johnson.

PANDALE CROSSING RESORT
RR 1024
Pandale, TX 78840
432–291–3210
432–559–7802 or 830–212–3783 (reservations)
www.pandalecrossing.com

Rustic cabins from $125.00 to $215.00 per night. Primitive camping available for $30.00 per night. Tube rental available at office.

The Chihuahuan Trail

US 90, Del Rio west through Val Verde County, about 80 miles

Driving west of Del Rio, travelers are in the Chihuahuan Desert. Be sure to fill up with gas and buy other essentials before leaving Del Rio because there are few gas stations or places to eat for the next 200 miles. Take a good look at the desert and the canyons along the way, which appear like jagged, unexpected splits in the earth. The Rio Grande and Mexico are on your left. Imagine riding in a stagecoach or a steam train along this way from Del Rio or San Antonio all the way to El Paso. It will make you really appreciate air conditioning.

Many long-distance bike riders cycle US 90, the southwesternmost route of the United States Bicycle Route System. Watch for cyclists all along US 90, and be kind to bikes. There are some tough hills out there, not to mention sun and weather.

Long-distance cyclists bike along US 90, especially in spring. Photo by author.

You can learn about the history and ecology of this desert at the visitor center at Seminole Canyon State Park and Historic Site, 9 miles west of Comstock, and the Judge Roy Bean Visitor Center and Botanical Garden in Langtry. In addition to the state park, Langtry, and Galloway White Shaman Preserve, which are covered in other chapters, this trail has numerous major places of interest along the way.

Travelers have been following this east-west trail since ancient times. Certainly native people 4,000 years ago knew the route from Las Moras Springs near Brackettville to San Felipe Springs in what is today Del Rio and beyond to springs farther west that are totally dry today. The Apaches and Comanches undoubtedly traveled that same route from the 1700s until the late 1880s.

The stagecoach route from San Antonio to El Paso in the 1800s used this trail and regularly stopped at various springs to rest. The US Army patrolled the road from about 1850 to protect the stage from Indian depredation. When the railroad came to this area in the 1880s, the rail lines also followed this same path. The first US 90 was built in 1927; it stretched from Van Horn in West Texas into eastern Louisiana and has been constantly maintained and expanded ever since.

BOQUILLAS EAGLE FORD SHALE ROAD CUTS

US 90 at various places

Appearing as bands of orange and white stone in the cuts along the highway are Upper Cretaceous geological strata that formed millions of years ago when much of Texas was a shallow sea. These cuts expose the Boquillas Eagle Ford Shale, one of the most prolific oil- and gas-producing formations in North America. Over a million barrels of crude oil a day have been produced from this shale, where it burrows down hundreds of feet in the earth of South Texas. The orange stone is the shale, and the white is limestone. Be careful, as drivers may encounter geology students walking along the highway studying the formations. These unusual geologic features are rarely seen anywhere else.

Boquillas Eagle Ford Shale rises to the surface west of Del Rio. Photo by Thomas C. Self.

US BORDER PATROL

US 90, just east of Comstock

If ever there was a border station on the front line of stopping illegal crossings and smuggling, it is the station in Comstock. Located less than 10 miles from the Rio Grande border with Mexico, this station finds itself in a high-traffic corridor for smuggling both illegal drugs and people. Mind your behavior in this area. The Comstock Station was founded back in 1925, with new facilities only recently completed.

Currently, the Comstock Station is responsible for ensuring and maintaining border security within a specified region of the international border separating the United States and Mexico. Border integrity is accomplished by constant vigilance of the immediate border and by detecting and apprehending subjects responsible for illegal incursions into the United States.

The Comstock Station utilizes a variety of means and methods to deter, detect, and interdict border penetrations, including marine patrol operations, ground patrol operations, traffic inspections, intelligence collection, and the deployment of technology. The Comstock Station area of responsibility encompasses 2,400 square miles, including 82 miles of international border. The international border is defined by the vast expanse of Lake Amistad and the Rio Grande.

Don't be surprised by a giant blimp patrolling the skies near the Rio Grande border as well. These blimps are part of the Tethered Aerostat Radar System, or TARS. They are used by US Customs and Border Protection. Their mission is to help agents and officers scan the skies for suspicious aircraft activity along the border. Blimps are almost 210 feet long, or about 20 feet longer than the Goodyear blimp. The blimps use high-powered radar, combined with information airplanes transmit to air traffic control, to monitor low-flying aircraft near the border while they are floating up to 12,000 feet in the air. These balloons have been used by the government for the past thirty years.

The new Comstock Border Patrol Complex consists of a Border Patrol Station, a vehicle checkpoint, vehicle wash building, maintenance building, refueling station, indoor firing range, short-stay kennel for Border Patrol canines, parking, and a helicopter landing pad.

PECOS RIVER HIGH BRIDGE OVERLOOK

US 90, about 50 miles west of Del Rio

Driving west from Del Rio, turn south from US 90 just before reaching the bridge and go uphill to reach this spectacular viewing spot. Watch carefully for a small sign indicating the overlook along the highway. Parking is also available in the turnout on the north side just before crossing the bridge if you miss the turn. Look north up the canyon beyond the bridge. Hidden just out of view in a large ravine is the White Shaman rock art site. Look south to see the mouth of the Pecos River, usually choked with weeds, as it empties

"Pecos Bill" Shafter

Lt. Col. William Rufus Shafter led five companies of cavalry and Black Seminole scouts from Fort Clark in pursuit of Lipan Indian warriors deep into the mountains of northern Coahuila, Mexico, in 1876–78. The cavalry established a base camp near the mouth of the Pecos River. From there they relentlessly attacked Indians who had been raiding in Texas. Shafter implemented the aggressive US policy toward Indians and increased tensions with Mexico over his border activities. Sometime later a cowboy character called Pecos Bill became popular in the United States, but Shafter used this nickname first.

into the Rio Grande. Soldiers from Fort Clark, outnumbered four to one, fought Comanche raiders near this spot in 1875, resulting in three Medals of Honor for the men. Several other important things occurred near here, too.

PECOS RIVER HIGH BRIDGE

US 90, Pecos River High Bridge Overlook

The Southwestern Pacific Railroad built the first highway bridge to span the river about one mile downriver from here in 1923. Just 50 feet above water, the 1923 bridge was destroyed by floodwaters in 1954. Two temporary low-water bridges, built nearby in 1954 and 1955, also were destroyed by floodwaters. A new 1,310-foot-long bridge was completed here in 1957. At 273 feet above the river, it is the highest highway bridge in Texas.

The High Bridge over the Pecos River offers a spectacular view. Photo by Jack Johnson.

SILVER SPIKE HISTORICAL MARKER

US 90, Pecos River High Bridge Overlook

Just as the Golden Spike joined the first US transcontinental railroad in Utah in 1869, a silver spike was used to join the two railroads building the southwestern transcontinental route on January 12, 1883, on the west side of the Pecos River near the overlook. The actual site is on private property and not open to the public. The Galveston, Harrisonburg and San Antonio Railroad, which later become the first part of the Southwestern Pacific rail system, joined two tracks together. One group of workers laid track from El Paso east, and another from San Antonio west. The Sunset Route, as it was called, met on the west bank of the Pecos River.

Pecos River Patty —*Howard "Jack" Thorp, 1901*

Where the Pecos River winds and turns in its journey to the sea,
From its white walls of sand and rock striving ever to be free,
Near the highest railroad bridge that all these modern times have seen,
Dwells fair young Patty Moorhead, the Pecos River Queen.

She's known by all the cowboys on the Pecos River wide,
They know full well that she can shoot, that she can rope, and she can ride;
She goes to every round-up, every cow-work without fail,
Looking out for all her cattle branded "walking hog on a rail."

She made her start in cattle, yes, made it with her rope;
Can tie down e'ry maverick 'fore it can strike a lope;
She can rope and tie and brand it as quick as any man;
She's voted by all cowboys an A-1 top cow-hand.

Across the Comstock railroad bridge, the highest in the West,
Patty rode her horse one day a lover's heart to test;
For he told her he would gladly risk all dangers for her sake,
But the puncher wouldn't follow, so she's still without a mate.

Temporary Chinese workers and other immigrants did the hard work of building the rail line through the hot, dry desert of Texas. Photo by Jack Johnson.

VINEGARROON HISTORICAL MARKER

US 90, about 10 miles east of Langtry

Vinegarroon, the largest of the temporary camps for railroad workers, was located west of this crossing of the Pecos River from 1881 to 1883. The tent city boasted a population of about 2,000 at one time. At its height, there were several stores and restaurants, a bakery, two barber shops, twenty-three saloons (including one owned by Roy Bean), a dance hall, a justice of the peace office, and a company of Texas Rangers. The place has been called "one of the wickedest tent villages the West had ever known."

Vinegarroon is also important because it was one of the first Chinese communities in Texas. Chinese men were employed in building the last stretch of railroad through Val Verde County in 1882. The men came, without wives or families, primarily from Guangdong, then known as Canton in English. The vast majority returned to China after 1883 because the US Congress passed the Chinese Exclusion Act, which forbade immigration from China until its repeal in 1943.

Accounts say the men worked seven days a week, twelve to sixteen hours per day. They were paid about $1.00 per day, which was about a third less than the wages of other workers. The work consisted primarily of shoveling by hand, grading, and surfacing prior to laying tracks. Some accounts claim the Chinese men were healthier than others because they bathed daily and drank tea made with boiled water. They ate rice, fish, pork, beef, and vegetables cooked in their own camps and lived in tents. Fragments of Chinese porcelain bowls and pipes are displayed at Seminole Canyon State Park and Historic Site as well as remains of hearths and bake ovens.

European immigrants from Germany, Italy, and Ireland worked with others from Mexico as well as African Americans and Anglos to build the line coming from the east. Their main camp, now completely gone, was near the Devils River. This group was primarily involved in laying track along the line, while Chinese workers for the Southwestern Pacific built the grade.

Dead Man's Trail

TX 163, Comstock to Ozona, about 82 miles

The first half of this route, going north, is slow and twisty, with numerous points of interest. Beyond Juno the road straightens out for an easy drive to Ozona. Many an Indian fight took place along this route.

> **Extreme Sports**
>
> Would you walk across a narrow railroad trestle thirty-two stories high without even a guardrail? Legend has it that a few fearless cowboys, perhaps emboldened with Judge Roy Bean's whiskey, occasionally rode their horses across the high Pecos River locomotive bridge to demonstrate their derring-do. We do not recommend this.—*Thanks to historian Mike Cox for this story*

DEAD MAN'S PASS

TX 163, about 10 miles north of Comstock

The first historical marker going north from Comstock is near a big gate for the Dead Man's Pass Ranch. Just a few miles off this road, steep gray canyons, now on private property, cut down to the Devils River. In the later half of the 1800s, when this was Comanche territory, wagon trains and other travelers were easily attacked near this spot. In one account, four men were killed, and in another, an entire family of five plus seven teamsters were massacred. Yet another story recounts an incident in 1860 when a wagon train was traveling through here at night. About three o'clock in the morning, a commotion caused the livestock to scatter, and some claimed the havoc was caused by Indians. Other claimed the animals were frightened by a panther or a bear or maybe a mountain lion. For many years this was considered the most dangerous place in Val Verde County.

DEAD MAN'S CREEK

Dead Man's Creek rises 1.5 miles southwest of Dead Man's Pass and runs southeast for 13 miles to its mouth on the Devils River. The creek was named for a traveling peddler who was robbed and killed by outlaws in a pass on the stream in the early 1880s. Reportedly the outlaws openly sold the stolen goods to railway workers. Judge Roy Bean in Langtry refused to hear the case because the robbery occurred east of the Pecos River and out of his jurisdiction. He was, after all, the "Law West of the Pecos."

Bigfoot Wallace

Legend has it that William Alexander Anderson Wallace (1817–99), a famous Texas Ranger better known as "Bigfoot," fought Comanches near Dead Man's Creek when he was protecting a westbound stagecoach sometime prior to 1870. The stage had stopped for lunch when it was attacked by Indians with guns as well as bows and arrows. The stage party successfully defended itself, even though it was a fierce battle, and returned to Fort Clark. A fast-selling book about Wallace was published in 1870 that recounted some of his many exploits.

BAKER'S CROSSING

TX 163, 21 miles north of Comstock

Large oak and pecan trees reach their roots deep into the flowing water of the Devils River here. This is a favorite put-in point for canoes and kayaks. There is a large parking pull-out area for kayakers where you can stop. The land around Baker's Crossing is private property, so this is not the place for a picnic, no matter how beautiful.

A small army post called Camp Hudson was established near Baker's Crossing in 1857 to protect travelers from San Antonio to El Paso on the Chihuahua Road. In 1859 part of the army's experimental Camel Corps from Camp Verde visited here. Perhaps you can imagine camels drinking from the stream. A post office opened in 1857 and closed in 1866. In 1871 Camp Hudson had three commissioned officers and sixty enlisted men. The camp was closed permanently in 1877 when the threat of Indian attacks had ceased. A historical marker is located in the 400 block of Pecan Street in Del Rio.

About 3 miles from Baker's Crossing, high in the cliffs, is a place called Baker Cave, which was occupied for thousands of years. The oldest deposits have been dated by archaeologists to 9,000 years ago, and the youngest are from about AD 900. The people ate fish, birds, rodents, and many plants such as sotol, lechugilla, yucca, prickly pear cactus, walnuts, pecans, persimmons, and grapes. Baker Cave is located on private property and is not open to visitors.

Purple Sage, or cenizo, can turn a dry desert into an ocean of lavender flowers. Photo by author.

HOOD'S DEVILS RIVER INDIAN FIGHT HISTORICAL MARKER

TX 163 at junction with RR 189, about 42 miles north of Comstock

Lt. John Bell Hood, who later gained fame during the Civil War, led a small US Army unit from Fort Mason in pursuit of Comanches near the Devils River in July 1857. The men were almost out of water, and many were suffering from heat exhaustion when they encountered a group of Indians waving a white flag. As Hood approached, the Indians attacked. Other Indians appeared from behind a ridge with lances and arrows. Comanche women set fire to the brush, adding to the confusion and danger. The fierce hand-to-hand battle killed two US Army men and wounded five, including Hood, who was shot through the hand with an arrow. He pulled it out and continued fighting. According to Hood, about ten Comanches were killed and nine wounded. The Indians retreated amidst the wails of the women as they cut their breasts and hair in mourning. Late that night a contingent from Camp Hudson arrived to care for the wounded soldiers and reinforce the beleaguered unit.

10

Movies

The landscape of Southwest Texas has provided a magnificent backdrop for hundreds of movies and many episodes of TV shows. At least 100 were filmed near Brackettville in an authentic replica of the Alamo known as Alamo Village, now closed. There have been many films and TV shows about Judge Roy Bean as well. Actor Matthew McConaughey, born in Uvalde in 1969, later starred in a film about the Newton brothers, notorious criminals also from Uvalde.

Historic buildings in Bracketteville have witnessed the rough and tumble Wild West. Photo by Thomas C. Self.

Here are my lists of selected movies of Southwest Texas. Enjoy!

Movies of the Western Hill Country

Year	Title	Actors and Director	Comments
2010	*Seven Days in Utopia*	Robert Duvall, Lucas Black, Kathy Baker. Directed by Matt Russell.	Filmed in Uvalde and Fredericksburg.
2007	*Road to El Paso*	Directed by Shiloh Richter.	Indie film partly filmed in Uvalde.
1997	*Once Upon a Time in China and America*	Jet Li, Rosamund Kwan. Directed by Sammo Hung.	Comic martial arts movie filmed at Alamo Village near Brackettville.
1994	*Gambler V: Playing for Keeps* (TV movie)	Kenny Rogers, Reba McEntire. Directed by Jack Bender.	Last in a series of five films based on the same character; filmed at Alamo Village near Brackettville, Uvalde, and other Texas locations.
1998	*The Newton Boys*	Matthew McConaughey, Ethan Hawke, Juliana Marguiles, Dwight Yoakum. Directed by Richard Linklater.	Based on a true story. Filmed in the Austin area.

Movies of the Lower Pecos Canyonlands

Year	Title	Actors and Directors	Comments
2007	*No Country for Old Men*	Tommy Lee Jones, Javier Bardem. Written and directed by Joel and Ethan Cohen.	Winner of four Academy Awards, including Best Picture. Partly filmed in Piedras Negras, Mexico, Del Rio, and Eagle Pass.
1996	*Lone Star*	Chris Cooper, Elizabeth Peña, Kris Kristofferson, Matthew McConaughey. Directed by John Sayles.	Nominated for four Academy Awards. Filmed in Del Rio, Eagle Pass, and Laredo.
1995	*Desperado*	Antonio Banderas, Salma Hayek. Directed by Richard Rodriquez.	Filmed in Ciudad Acuña, Mexico.
1993	*Like Water for Chocolate*	Lumi Cavazos, Marco Leonardi.	Filmed in Ciudad Acuña and Piedras Negras, Mexico, as well as Del Rio. Won Mexico's Ariel Award for Best Picture and was the highest-grossing Spanish language film ever released in the United States at that time.
1993	*Mariachi*	Carlos Gallardo, Consuela Gomez. Written and directed by Robert Rodriquez.	Shot for $7,000 with mostly amateur actors in Ciudad Acuña, Mexico. This was Robert Rodriguez's film debut.

1974	*The Sugarland Express*	Goldie Hawn, Ben Johnson. Directed by Steven Spielberg.	This is the first film written and directed by Steven Spielberg. Based on a true story, it was partly filmed in Del Rio. The film won Best Screenplay at Cannes.
1972	*The Life and Times of Judge Roy Bean*	Paul Newman, Victoria Principal, Anthony Perkins, Jacqueline Bisset. Directed by John Huston.	Loosely based on Judge Roy Bean's biography, the film won an Academy Award for Best Original Song.
1960	*The Alamo*	John Wayne, Richard Widmark. Directed by John Wayne.	This film was John Wayne's project all the way, and he even invested his own money in it. Filmed at the specially built set in Brackettville, the film was nominated for six Academy Awards and won for Best Sound.
1953	*Arrowhead*	Charlton Heston, Jack Palance. Directed by Charles Marquis Warren.	Filmed in Brackettville at Fort Clark and on local ranches.
1940	*The Westerner*	Gary Cooper, Walter Brennan. Directed by William Wyler.	Brennan won Best Supporting Actor for his portrayal of Judge Roy Bean. Filmed in Arizona.

You Can Help

Edible fruits hang on a yucca plant in Southwest Texas. Photo by the author.

You can help preserve the fragile and irreplaceable natural and cultural sites listed in this guide by donating to any of the following:

The Nature Conservancy

a nonprofit 501(C)3

www.nature.org/membership-giving/donation/index.htm

Shumla School

a nonprofit 501(C)3

www.shumla.org

Texas Beyond History

www.texasbeyondhistory.net

Texas Historical Commission

www.thc.state.tx.us/get-involved

Texas Parks and Wildlife Department

www.tpwd.texas.gov/business/donations/

Tricky Travel Trivia

All questions are answered in this guide.

1. Where can you see piñon pines?
2. What infamous gang of train robbers lived in Uvalde?
3. Where can you see a 4,000-year-old painting?
4. Buffalo soldiers were stationed at what three forts?
5. When was the southwestern route of the transcontinental railway completed?
6. Why did the US Army build a string of forts along the Rio Grande?
7. Where can you see bigtooth maples?
8. Where can you see a painting by an Old World Master?
9. What desert is partly located in Southwest Texas?
10. Who are the Kickapoo Indians?
11. Who owned a powerful border radio station?
12. Where can you learn about plants of the Chihuahuan Desert?
13. Who did the hard labor of building the southwestern railroads?
14. What is the highest bridge in Texas?
15. Where does the Rio Grande start?
16. Which state park has at least twenty caves?
17. Where is one of the oldest construction projects in North America?
18. Where can you swim in the third-largest spring-fed swimming pool in Texas?
19. Immigrants from what country started vineyards near Del Rio?
20. What kind of trees grow near Quemado?
21. Who was Cal Rodgers?
22. Where is the largest bull-riding event in the United States?
23. Who once landed on Main Street in Camp Wood?

24. How is the Cuban missile crisis of 1962 connected to Del Rio?
25. Name someone born in Uvalde.
26. What town is currently underwater?
27. Where is Judge Roy Bean's saloon?
28. Where might you see a blimp?
29. Who was Wolfman Jack?
30. What movie shot in Southwest Texas won four Academy awards?

Multiple Choice

1. The first airplane to fly across the entire United States from east to west was:
   A. the *Lucky Lindy*
   B. the U-2
   C. the *Vin Fiz*
2. The Kickapoo Indians own:
   A. Kickapoo Caverns
   B. Lucky Eagle Casino
   C. First State Bank
3. Which of the following is considered a ghost town?
   A. Eagle Pass
   B. Juno
   C. Concan
4. Which of the following was governor of Texas?
   A. Dolph Briscoe
   B. John Brinkley
   C. June Carter
5. Who won the Medal of Honor?
   A. Dolph Briscoe
   B. Pompey Factor
   C. Bigfoot Wallace
6. Who was the "Law West of the Pecos?"
   A. John Bell Hood
   B. Pecos River Patty
   C. Judge Roy Bean

7. Where is geocaching popular?
    A. Pecos River
    B. Devil's Sinkhole
    C. Garner State Park
8. What is "leaf-peeping"?
    A. looking at colored leaves in autumn
    B. spying endangered plants
    C. looking up at trees while floating down the river
9. What town calls itself the "Angora goat capital of the world?"
    A. Pumpville
    B. Leakey
    C. Rocksprings
10. What do Mexican free-tailed bats eat?
    A. prickly pear
    B. insects
    C. minnows
11. The Hole in the Wall gang was also known by what name?
    A. the Newton Boys
    B. the Pecos Rangers
    C. the Wild Bunch
12. Why did Dr. Brinkley originally gain notoriety?
    A. He did the first heart transplant.
    B. He transplanted goat glands into men.
    C. He discovered that prickly pear cactus is great in Jello shots.
13. Where can you see reenactments of shooting, cooking, tenting, and other aspects of daily life in the 1850s?
    A. Fort Inge and Fort Clark
    B. Museum of the Army
    C. Longhorn Museum
14. What does *frio* mean in English?
    A. long
    B. nuts
    C. cold

15. What did Butch Cassidy and the Sundance Kid do?
    A. rob trains
    B. build railroads
    C. discover canyons
16. Where could bat guano be mined?
    A. under the Amistad bridge
    B. in the Devil's Sinkhole
    C. among the boulders in the Nueces River
17. Where can you see an opera house?
    A. Uvalde
    B. Eagle Pass
    C. Del Rio
18. Where was the actor Matthew McConaughey born?
    A. Austin
    B. Uvalde
    C. San Antonio
19. What three rivers run through the Western Hill Country?
    A. Frio, Rio Grande, and Nueces
    B. Columbia, Pecos, and Sabinal
    C. Nueces, Frio, and Sabinal
20. Where is the third-largest spring-fed pool in Texas?
    A. Fort Clark
    B. Fort Inge
    C. Fort Lancaster

For Further Reading

Aulbach, Louis F. *The Devils River: Baker's Crossing to the Rough Canyon Marina, Maps and Notes for River Runners*. Houston, TX: Wilderness Area Map Service, 2005.

Aulbach, Louis F., and Jack Richardson. *The Lower Pecos River: Pandale to Lake Amistad, Maps and Notes for River Runners*. 2nd ed. Houston, TX: Wilderness Area Map Service, 2008.

Black, Mary S. *Peyote Fire: Shaman of the Canyons*. Austin, TX: Writers Press, 2015.

Britten, Thomas A. *A Brief History of the Black Seminole Indian Scouts*. Lewiston, NY: Edwin Mellen Publishers, 1999.

Boyd, Carolyn. *Rock Art of the Lower Pecos*. College Station, TX: Texas A&M University Press, 2003.

Dodson, Carolyn, and Robert DeWitt Ivey. *A Guide to Plants of the Northern Chihuahuan Desert*. Albuquerque: University of New Mexico Press, 2012.

Fowler, Gene, and Bill Crawford. *Border Radio: Quacks, Yodelers, Pitchmen, Psychics, and Other Amazing Broadcasters of the American Airwaves*. Austin: University of Texas Press, 2002.

Harveson, Louis A. *Woody Plants of the Big Bend and Trans-Pecos: A Field Guide to Common Browse for Wildlife*. College Station: Texas A&M University Press, 2016.

LaTorre, Felipe A., and Dolores L. LaTorre. *The Mexican Kickapoo Indians*. Mineola, NY: Dover Publications, 2012.

LeBow, Eileen F. *Cal Rodgers and the Vin Fiz: The First Transcontinental Flight*. Washington, DC: Smithsonian Institution Press, 1989.

Mock, Shirley Boteler. *Dreaming with the Ancestors: Black Seminole Women in Texas and Mexico*. Norman: University of Oklahoma Press, 2010.

Newton, Willis, and Joe Newton. *The Newton Boys: Portrait of an Outlaw Gang*. Austin, TX: State House Press, 1994.

Shafer, Harry J. *Ancient Texans: Rock Art and Lifeways along the Lower Pecos*. Houston, TX: Gulf Publishing Company, 1986.

Sheffer, Debra J. *The Buffalo Soldiers: Their Epic Story and Major Campaigns*. Westport, CT: Praeger, 2015.

Skiles, Jack. *Judge Roy Bean Country*. Lubbock: Texas Tech University Press, 1996.

Texas Beyond History. "Lower Pecos Canyonlands." www.texasbeyondhistory.net/Pecos/.

Index

Alamo Village, 91
Amistad Reservoir, or Lake Amistad, 29–31
Amistad National Recreation Area, 38–40
Angora goat, 144
Aviation History Trail, 184

Barksdale, 88–89
Bat Trail, 183
Battle of the Nueces, 24
Baxter's Curve Train Robbery, 178
Bean, Judge Roy Visitor Center and Botanical Garden, 172–174
Black Seminole Indian Scouts, 2, 72, 75, 92, 182, 190
bird-watching, 12, 44, 56–57, 86, 96, 105, 138, 157, 186
Bigfoot Wallace, 195
Brackettville, 89–95
Brinkley, Dr. John R., 117
Briscoe, Dolph, 152, 155
Briscoe-Garner Museum, 155
Briscoe, Janey Slaughter Grand Opera House, 156
border radio, 117
Bowie, Jim Silver Mine, 158
Buffalo Soldiers, 74
Buffalo Soldiers and Black Seminole Indian Scouts Trail, 182
Bullhead Canyon Trail, 182

Camp Dix, C.S.A., 80
Camp Wood, 95–100
camping, 39, 40, 49–50, 52–53, 56, 60, 95, 100
Carta Valley, 170
Carter Family, 113
Chihuahuan Desert, 26–29
Chihuahuan Trail, 187
Chinese workers, 193
Comstock, 101–102
Concan, 103–111
"coon can," 103
Ciudad Acuña, 113–114
Cuban Missile Crisis, 114

Dead Man's Trail, 193
Del Rio, 111–127
Devils River, 32–34
Devils River State Natural Area, 41–42
Devils River (ghost town), 170
Devil's Sinkhole State Natural Area, 42–44
Dolores, 170

Eagle Pass, 128–135
El Indio, 136
European immigrants, 116, 193

extreme sports, 194

First US Military Cross-Country Flight, 78
Fort Clark, 72–76
Fort Duncan, 77–78
Fort Inge, 78–80
Frio River, 20–23

Garner, John Nance, 45, 152, 154
Garner State Park, 44–51
Galloway White Shaman Preserve, 70–71
geocaching, 52
Great Train Robbery Trail, 185

hiking, 48, 53, 57, 59

Juno, 171

Kickapoo Cavern State Park, 54–57
Kickapoo Lucky Eagle Casino, 129–130

Laguna, 172
Langtry, 172–176
Leakey, 136–143
Lindbergh, Charles, 96
Las Moras Springs and Creek, 31
Lost Maples State Natural Area, 51–53
Lower Pecos Canyonlands, 7–9, 26

McConaughey, Matthew, 152, 186, 197–199
McLaurin Raid, 137
Montell, 176–177

New Money and Old Art Trail, 182
Newton Boys, 153
Normandy, 143
Nueces River, 23–25

"Pecos Bill" Shafter, 190
Pecos Crossing Trail, 186
Pecos River, 33–34
Pecos River High Bridge, 190–191
Pecos River Patty, 192
Piedras Negras, 130
Pumpville, 177

Quemado, 143

Rattlin' Rodge, 105
Rio Grande, 34–36
Robinson Massacre, 164
Rocksprings, 144–148
Rodgers, Cal, 184

Sabinal River, 25
San Felipe Springs, 36–37
Seminole Canyon State Park and Historic Site, 58–60, 67–70
Shumla, 179

Tips for a Successful Tubing Float Trip, 47
Twisted Sisters Trail, 180–181

Utopia, 148–152
Uvalde, 152–164
US Border Patrol, 189

Vanderpool, 165–168
Vin Fiz, 184
Vinegarroon, 193

Western Hill Country, 4–7, 20
White Shaman, see Galloway White Shaman Preserve
Windus, Claron Augustus, 76
Wolfman Jack, 119

Other Books in the Tarleton State University Southwestern Studies in the Humanities Series

In the Deep Heart's Core: Reflections on Life, Letters, and Texas
Craig E. Clifford

Cannibals and Condos: Texans and Texas along the Gulf Coast
Robert L. Maril

Rough and Rowdy Ways: The Life and Hard Times of Edward Anderson
Patrick Bennett

Larry McMurtry and the Victorian Novel
Roger W. Jones

Nueva Granada: Paul Horgan and the Southwest
Robert F. Gish

Beautiful Swift Fox: Erna Fergusson and the Modern Southwest
Robert F. Gish

Texas Women Writers: A Tradition of Their Own
Sylvia A. Grider and Lou H. Rodenberger

Riding the Wind and Other Tales
James Hoggard

State of Mind: Texas Literature and Culture
Tom Pilkington

Culture in the American Southwest: The Earth, the Sky, the People
Keith L. Bryant

Donald Barthelme: The Genesis of a Cool Sound
Helen M. Barthelme

West of the American Dream: An Encounter with Texas
Paul Christensen

San Antonio on Parade: Six Historic Festivals
Judith B. Sobré

Let's Hear It: Stories by Texas Women Writers
Sylvia A. Grider and Lou H. Rodenberger

Lone Star Chapters: The Story of Texas Literary Clubs
Betty H. Wiesepape

Pastoral Vision of Cormac McCarthy
Georg Guillemin

Exploding the Western: Myths of Empire on the Postmodern Frontier
Sara L. Spurgeon

Undaunted: A Norwegian Woman in Frontier Texas
Charles H. Russell

Lost Years of William S. Burroughs: Beats in South Texas
Robert E. Johnson

Birth of a Texas Ghost Town: Thurber, 1886–1933
Mary J. Gentry and Lindsay T. Baker

Alexandre Hogue: An American Visionary—Paintings and Works on Paper
Susie Kalil

Fritos® Pie: Stories, Recipes, and More
Kaleta Doolin

Faded Glory: A Century of Forgotten Texas Military Sites, Then and Now
Thomas E. Alexander and Dan K. Utley

Marfa Flights: Aerial Views of Big Bend Country
Paul V. Chaplo

Still Turning: A History of Aermotor Windmills
Christopher C. Gillis